Glencoe Literature
The Reader's Choice

Leveled Vocabulary Development

Adapted
British Literature

McGraw Hill Glencoe

New York, New York   Columbus, Ohio   Chicago, Illinois   Peoria, Illinois   Woodland Hills, California

Mc Graw Hill **Glencoe**

Send all inquiries to:
Glencoe/McGraw-Hill
8787 Orion Place
Columbus, OH 43240-4027

ISBN-13: 978-0-07-876872-9
ISBN-10: 0-07-876872-1

Printed in the United States of America.

2 3 4 5 6 7 8 9 047 12 11 10 09 08 07

Table of Contents

UNIT 3   From Puritanism to the Enlightenment (1640–1780)

UNIT 4 The Triumph of Romanticism (1750–1837)

UNIT 5 The Victorian Age (1837–1901)

UNIT 6　The Modern Age (1901–1950)

UNIT 7　An International Literature (1950–Present)

Vocabulary Development

from Beowulf *Translated by* BURTON RAFFEL

Selection Vocabulary

lament (lə ment′) *n.* expression of sorrow; song or literary composition that mourns a loss or death

forged (fôrjd) *adj.* formed or shaped, often with blows or pressure after heating

shroud (shroud) *n.* burial cloth

infamous (in′fə məs) *adj.* having a bad reputation; notorious

writhing (rîth əng) *adj.* twisting, as in pain

EXERCISE A   Determining Meaning

For each sentence below, write the selection vocabulary word that belongs in the blank.

1. The worm was _____ on the fishing hook.

2. The mummy was buried with a woven _____.

3. The shopkeeper had become _____ for trying to cheat his customers.

4. The saddest song in the opera was the _____ after the hero was killed.

5. The sword looked new though it was _____ centuries ago.

EXERCISE B   Practice with Synonyms and Antonyms

Additional Vocabulary

purge (purj) *v.* to free of something unwanted

venom (ven′ əm) *n.* material that is poisonous, usually from an animal

comrade (kom′ rad) *n.* an intimate friend; a fellow soldier

Choose the correct synonym or antonym for each additional vocabulary word.

1. Which word is a synonym for **venom**?
   A. deadly   **B.** antidote   **C.** poison   **D.** danger

2. Which word is an antonym for **comrade**?
   A. enemy   **B.** stranger   **C.** companion   **D.** friend

3. Which word is a synonym for **purge**?
   A. collect   **B.** rid   **C.** develop   **D.** chase

Name _____ Class _____ Date _____

Vocabulary Development

The Seafarer *Translated by* BURTON RAFFEL

Selection Vocabulary

admonish (ad mon′ ish) *v.* to warn; to reprimand

rancor (rang′ kər) *n.* bitter malice or resentment

flourish (flur′ ish) *v.* to exist at the peak of development or achievement; to thrive

blanch (blanch) *v.* to turn white or become pale

EXERCISE A   Applying Meaning

Write the selection vocabulary word that best answers each question.

1. What does someone do when their face turns pale? _____

2. What does a flower do when it blooms beautifully? _____

3. What is a feeling of bitterness? _____

4. What does someone do when they issue a warning? _____

EXERCISE B   Using Context Clues

Additional Vocabulary

misfortune (mis fôr′ chən) *n.* a distressing or unfortunate incident or event

oath (ōth) *n.* a solemn promise or declaration of truth

toil (toil) *n.* laborious effort

wither (with′ ər) *v.* to shrivel; to lose vitality or freshness

Choose the best meaning of the boldfaced additional vocabulary word. Circle your answer.

1. The fire caused great **misfortune** for the family because they lost everything they had.

   A. disagreement   **B.** danger   **C.** hardship

2. The hot sun and lack of water caused the plants to **wither**.

   A. dry up   **B.** grow   **C.** flourish

3. After many days of **toil**, which left him exhausted, Larry succeeded in building a boat.

   A. patience   **B.** work   **C.** boredom

4. Ginny swore an **oath** that she would do everything possible to help her friend.

   A. aid   **B.** decision   **C.** promise

Vocabulary Development

from The Ecclesiastical History of the English People

THE VENERABLE BEDE

Selection Vocabulary

expound (iks pound′) *v.* to set forth in detail, explain
diligently (dil′ ə jənt lē) *adv.* persistently
aspire (əs pīr′) *v.* to strive for
frivolous (friv′ə ləs) *adj.* not serious; silly

EXERCISE A Determining Meaning

For each sentence below, write the selection vocabulary word that belongs in the blank.

1. Working _____ on the science project paid off; we won the state competition!

2. She acts in such a _____ manner, always laughing at serious times.

3. I _____ to be an engineer because I love to see how things work inside.

4. Our history teachers would often _____ the details of the causes of World War I.

EXERCISE B Classifying

The word box below contains words that can be grouped according to their meanings. Select the words with similar definitions and place them beneath the proper selection vocabulary term heading.

| industriously explain seek trivial thoroughly develop |
| aim silly attentively expand desire thoughtless |

expound	diligently	aspire	frivolous
_____	_____	_____	_____
_____	_____	_____	_____
_____	_____	_____	_____

EXERCISE C Responding to the Selection

Use the back of this sheet to write four sentences using at least two of the selection vocabulary words. In each sentence, explore some historical fact, event, or person.

Vocabulary Development
from **The Canterbury Tales,** *from* **The Prologue**

GEOFFREY CHAUCER

Selection Vocabulary

solicitous (sə lis′ ə təs) *adj.* full of concern
estimable (es′tə mə bəl) *adj.* deserving of esteem; admirable
discreet (dis krēt′) *adj.* having or showing careful judgment in speech and
   action; prudent
disdainful (dis dān′ fəl) *adj.* feeling or showing contempt; scornful
prevarication (pri var′ ə kā′ shən) *n.* the act of evading the truth; lying

EXERCISE A   Determining Meaning

In each space below, write the selection vocabulary word that best completes each sentence.

1. The _____ man stormed from the meeting to show his scorn for the speaker.

2. He's quite _____, so the rash behavior you accuse him of is hard to believe.

3. He's an _____ politician whom voters respect.

4. It was with much _____ that Mr. Smith dealt with the accusations.

5. Some say she's kind and _____, but I think she's nosey.

EXERCISE B   Classifying

Draw a line to connect each vocabulary word to the group of words associated with it. Use a dictionary for help.

1. discreet	**A.** kind, caring, considerate
2. prevarication	**B.** scornful, mocking, aloof
3. solicitous	**C.** careful, cautious, prudent
4. disdainful	**D.** good, worthy, admirable
5. estimable	**E.** deception, distortion, forgery

EXERCISE C   Responding to the Selection

On the back of this sheet, use three vocabulary words to describe some of the characters.

Vocabulary Development

from The Canterbury Tales, *from* The Pardoner's Tale

GEOFFREY CHAUCER

Selection Vocabulary

adversary (ad′ vər ser′ ē) *n.* opponent; enemy
prudent (prōōd′ ənt) *adj.* cautious; careful
gratify (grat′ e fī′) *v.* to satisfy; indulge
deftly (deft lē) *adv.* skillfully; nimbly

EXERCISE A   Determining Meaning

For each sentence below, write the selection vocabulary word that best completes the sentence.

1. He didn't know how to wait, but would always want to _____ his wishes immediately.

2. Her _____ in the chess competition was intelligent, thoughtful, and deliberate.

3. When she worked at the pottery wheel, she moved her hands _____ and expertly.

4. It would be _____ to write down your phone number so we can call you in an emergency.

EXERCISE B   Using Context Clues

Use context clues to identify the selection vocabulary word that best completes each sentence.

1. The crying baby was impossible to _____; she refused to be comforted by anyone.

2. The skier raced _____ and skillfully through the slalom gates.

3. My biggest enemy, a childhood _____, surprisingly came to my rescue.

4. What a _____ child she is—I've never known a four year old to behave so cautiously.

EXERCISE C   Responding to the Selection

On the back of this sheet, use three of the vocabulary words to write a summary of the events in the selection.

Name _____ Class _____ Date _____

Vocabulary Development

from The Canterbury Tales, *from* The Wife of Bath's Tale

GEOFFREY CHAUCER

Selection Vocabulary

reprove (ri prōōv′) *v.* to scold or correct, usually gently or out of kindness
concede (kən sēd′) *v.* to admit as true; acknowledge
disperse (dispurs′) *v.* to scatter about; distribute widely
arrogance (ar′ ə gəns) *n.* overbearing pride or self-importance
suffice (sə fīs′) *v.* to be enough for

EXERCISE A   Determining Meaning

For each sentence below, write the selection vocabulary word that best completes the sentence.

1. The mother promised to _____ her son for his misbehavior the moment they got home.

2. "That will _____," said the customer to the butcher.

3. _____ won't get you very far in life—people appreciate humility.

4. The moment the mouse shows his whiskers, the children _____.

5. I _____ that I have not been a very good friend.

EXERCISE B   Practice with Synonyms

For each item below, choose the correct synonym for the selection vocabulary word in bold type.

1. We should **disperse** the flyers throughout campus so everyone knows about the meeting.
A. recall   **B.** contain   **C.** scatter   **D.** hold onto

2. The librarian would **reprove** her students who returned library books late.
A. celebrate   **B.** scold   **C.** congratulate   **D.** applaud

3. Although he always had good ideas, his personality was marred by **arrogance**.
A. kindness   **B.** friendliness   **C.** modesty   **D.** pride

4. For the purposes of our sewing project, these two bolts of fabric should **suffice**.
A. be enough   **B.** be not enough   **C.** be incorrect   **D.** be ready

5. Do you **concede** that you were partly responsible for losing the papers?
A. disagree   **B.** agree   **C.** argue   **D.** dispute

Vocabulary Development

from **The Book of Margery Kempe** MARGERY KEMPE

Selection Vocabulary

divulge (di vulj′) *v.* to make known; disclose
slander (slan′ dər) *v.* to utter false or malicious statements about
instigation (in′ stə gā′ shən) *n.* the act of inciting or urging on
restrain (ri strān′) *v.* to hold back; restrict
composure (kəm pō′ zhər) *n.* a calm or tranquil state of mind

EXERCISE A Determining Meaning

For each item below, write the selection vocabulary word that answers each question.

1. What do you do if you control yourself in a chaotic situation? _____

2. What is another word for someone saying bad things about you? _____

3. What is a synonym for telling a secret? _____

4. How would you describe the state of someone who is always calm? _____

5. What is another word for starting something? _____

EXERCISE B Classifying

Write the vocabulary word that best completes each group of related words.
Use a dictionary for help.

1. hold back, bring under control, contain, _____

2. reveal, make known, let drop, _____

3. self-control, calmness, serenity, _____

4. beginning, start, commencement, _____

5. insult, smear, slur, _____

EXERCISE C Responding to the Selection

On the back of this sheet, use three vocabulary words to write a paragraph that explains your personal feelings about what you have read from Margery Kempe's autobiography.

Name _____ Class _____ Date _____

Vocabulary Development

from Everyman ANONYMOUS

Selection Vocabulary

reckoning (rek′ ən ing) *n.* a settlement of accounts
perceive (pər sēv′) *v.* to become aware of; comprehend
respite (res′ pit) *n.* a delay or extension
adversity (advur′ să tē) *n.* a state of hardship; misfortune

EXERCISE A — Determining Meaning

In each space below, write the selection vocabulary word that best completes each sentence.

1. The family has survived much _____ and has used each hardship as a life lesson.

2. We needed hours to reach an accurate _____ after the bake sale.

3. I asked my professor for a _____ on the term paper.

4. I did not _____ the film as you did.

EXERCISE B — Practice with Synonyms and Antonyms

For each selection vocabulary word, circle its synonym and underline its antonym.

1. reckoning – weighing up/disregard

2. perceive – ignore/observe

3. respite – continuation/break

4. adversity – hardship/privilege

EXERCISE C — Responding to the Selection

On the back of this sheet, use three vocabulary words to write a summary of the selection.

Vocabulary Development

from **Sir Gawain and the Green Knight**

Translated by JOHN GARDNER

Selection Vocabulary

copiously (kō′ p ē əs lē) *adv.* plentifully
intrepid (in trep′ id) *adj.* fearless; courageous
dauntless (dont′ lis) *adj.* daring; not easily discouraged
blithe (blīth) *adj.* carefree; lighthearted

EXERCISE A Determining Meaning

In each space below, write the selection vocabulary word that completes the sentence.

1. He was _____ in his pursuit of the truth; no one could discourage him.

2. She took notes _____ in her science class so she would understand how the experiment worked.

3. The _____ explorer journeyed through the frozen environment without fear.

4. The beautiful summer day made us all feel _____ and relaxed.

EXERCISE B Applying Meaning

Additional Vocabulary

gruesome (grōō′ səm) *adj.* inspiring horror or repulsion
peril (per′ əl) *n.* exposure to the risk of being harmed
meager (mē′ gər) *adj.* deficient in quality or quantity
indebted (in det′ id) *adj.* owing gratitude or recognition to another
renowned (ri nound′) *adj.* celebrated; famous

Write the additional vocabulary word that best completes each sentence.

1. Steve felt _____ to his friend for all the help she had given him.

2. The dead fish washed up on the shore were a _____ sight.

3. Though used to eating more food, they began to become accustomed to the _____ portions.

4. The storm at sea put everyone on board in _____.

5. Helen became _____ for her excellent piano playing.

EXERCISE C Responding to the Selection

On the back of this sheet, use four of the vocabulary words to write a paragraph describing a knight's characteristics.

Name _____ Class _____ Date _____

Vocabulary Development

from **Le Morte d'Arthur** SIR THOMAS MALORY

Selection Vocabulary

doleful (dōl′ fəl) *adj.* sad
peril (per′ əl) *n.* risk of injury, loss or destruction
jeopardy (jep′ ər dē) *n.* danger
brandish (bran′ dish) *v.* to shake or swing threateningly, as a weapon

EXERCISE A   Determining Meaning

For each sentence below, write the selection vocabulary word that belongs in the blank.

1. The mountain climbers didn't realize the _____ they faced until the heavy snowstorm began.

2. Frank's _____ expression reflected how disappointed he was.

3. Because Caroline ignored common safety precautions, she put her family in _____.

4. Tom began to _____ his club to prove to his enemy how strong he was.

EXERCISE B   Understanding Homonyms

Additional Vocabulary

fair (fãr) *adj.* beautiful; just, unbiased
draw (drô) *v.* to pull out; to produce a likeness or representation of by making lines on a surface
leave (lēv) *v.* to go away from, *n.* permission
wind (wind) *n.* a natural movement of air

Read each sentence and then write down the meaning of the boldfaced word.

1. Jamie had to **leave** the theater before the end of the play. _____

2. My daughter likes to **draw** cats. _____

3. The strong **wind** caused many tree branches to fall. _____

4. It is important for a teacher to be **fair** when grading students. _____

5. The general ordered the soldiers to **draw** their swords. _____

EXERCISE C   Responding to the Selection

On the back of this sheet, use three vocabulary words to write a description of your favorite character from the selection. Explain what you like about this character and why.

Vocabulary Development

Sir Patrick Spens *and* Bonny Barbara Allan *and*

Get Up and Bar the Door ANONYMOUS

Selection Vocabulary

dwell (dwel) *v.* to live as a resident
foremost (fôr′ mōst) *adj.* ahead of all others or in the first position

EXERCISE A   Determining Meaning

In each space below, write the selection vocabulary word that belongs in the blank.

1. His safety was _____ in my mind, as I was responsible for all of the children that day.

2. When I grow up, I would love to _____ in a small village in the mountains.

EXERCISE B   Applying Meaning

Additional Vocabulary

deed (dēd) *n.* something that is done
tavern (tav′ ərn) *n.* establishment where alcoholic beverages are served; inn
gay (gā) *adj.* happily excited; lively

Write the additional vocabulary word that belongs in the blank.

1. The children were _____ as they looked forward to the trip.

2. The _____ serves lunch in the afternoons.

3. Kay considered the signing of the contract to be an important _____.

EXERCISE C   Responding to the Selection

On the back of this sheet, use three of the vocabulary words to write a paragraph describing a setting for one of these ballads.

Vocabulary Development

On Monsieur's Departure *and*

Speech to the Troops at Tilbury ELIZABETH I

Selection Vocabulary

mute (mūt) *adj.* unable to speak; refraining from producing vocal sounds
suppressed (sə prest′) *adj.* subdued; held back
treachery (treach′ ər ē) *n.* willful betrayal of trust; treason
concord (kon′ kôrd) *n.* an agreement of interests or feelings
valor (val′ ər) *n.* courage and boldness, as in battle; bravery

EXERCISE A | Determining Meaning

For each sentence below, write the selection vocabulary word that best
completes the sentence.

1. "I will not be _____!" Katie yelled at the club president after he
tried to stop her speech.

2. The act was a rare display of _____, and the queen was
impressed by his victory.

3. Josie stopped talking and remained _____ after her embarrassing
remark.

4. "In order to make this agreement work, we must have a _____,"
Tanner replied.

5. His _____ astounded her, and she wished they had never
become friends.

EXERCISE B | Classifying

Additional Vocabulary

grieve (grēv) *v.* to cause sorrow; have sadness over a loss
care (kār) *n.* mental suffering; unhappiness; sadness
stark (stark) *adj.* completely blunt; to an extreme

Write the vocabulary word that completes each group of related words. Use a
dictionary for help.

1. direct, severe, harsh, _____

2. mourn, suffer, cry, _____

3. concern, anxiety, worry, _____

EXERCISE C | Responding to the Selection

On the back of this sheet, use two selection vocabulary words to write a
paragraph summarizing the events of this selection.

Leveled Vocabulary Development, Adapted

Vocabulary Development

The Lover Showeth How He Is Forsaken SIR THOMAS WYATT

Selection Vocabulary

flee (flē) *v.* to run away
stalking (stôk′ ing) *v.* tracking; pursuing
meek (mēk) *adj.* mild; gentle
continual (kən tin′ ūəl) *adj.* ongoing; repeated
bitter (bit′ ər) *adj.* hard to bear; causing pain

EXERCISE A   Determining Meaning

For each sentence below, write the selection vocabulary word that best completes the sentence.

1. Her classmates described her as _____ and mild, but she was actually quite strong.

2. The antelope tried to _____ the lion, but unfortunately the lion was too fast.

3. Gym class was a _____ hour for José, because his sprained wrist kept him from playng basketball, his favorite sport.

4. As we moved through the forest, _____ the fox on horseback, I felt sorry for the creature.

5. The scratched CD was on a _____ loop, repeating the same song over and over again.

EXERCISE B   Determining Meaning

Use a dictionary to look up each of the following additional vocabulary words. Then complete the chart by writing the definition in the space provided.

Additional Vocabulary Word	Definition
fortune (fôr′ chən) *n.*	
chamber (chām′ bər) *n.*	
tame (tām) *adj.*	
unkindly (un kīnd lē) *adv.*	

EXERCISE C   Responding to the Selection

On the back of this sheet, use two selection vocabulary words to write an alternate ending to the selection. Your response may or may not rhyme.

UNIT 2

Vocabulary Development

Sonnet 30 *and* Sonnet 75 EDMUND SPENSER

Selection Vocabulary

congeal (kən jēl′) *v.* harden, thicken
vain (vān) *adj.* conceited, excessively pleased with oneself
mortal (môrt′ əl) *adj.* destined to die
subdue (səb dōō′) *v.* conquer; overcome; quiet

EXERCISE A   Determining Meaning

For each sentence below, write the selection vocabulary word that belongs in the blank.

1. Marcus tried to _____ his dog when it started barking at the cat.

2. The gravy began to _____ as it cooled in the pan.

3. Ashley was always saying how pretty she was; the other girls thought she was very _____.

4. Human beings are _____, so they will not live forever.

EXERCISE B   Classifying

Additional Vocabulary

devise (di vīz′) *v.* to plan
assay (ə sā′) *v.* to try
delayed (di lād′) *v.* lessened
entreat (en trêt′) *v.* to beg

Write the additional vocabulary word that belongs with each group of related words. Use a dictionary for help.

1. plead, beg, ask, _____

2. attempt, endeavor, try, _____

3. reduced, lessened, decreased, _____

4. prepare, arrange, plot, _____

EXERCISE C   Responding to the Selection

On the back of this sheet, use four vocabulary words to describe the main speaker in the selection.

Leveled Vocabulary Development, Adapted

Vocabulary Development

Sonnet 31 *and* Sonnet 39 SIR PHILIP SIDNEY

Selection Vocabulary

wan (won) *adj.* pale
languish (lang′ gwish) *adj.* to be dispirited; to lack vitality
deem (dēm) *v.* to regard as, consider
scorn (skôrn) *v.* to reject as contemptible or unworthy
balm (bäm) *n.* a healing ointment; a soothing application

EXERCISE A   Determining Meaning

For each sentence below, write the selection vocabulary word that belongs in
the blank.

1. I would _____ your opinion valid if you could come up with
some reasons to support it.

2. The doctor suggested using an aloe vera _____ to help heal the
burn on your arm.

3. She looked _____ and ashen when confronted with the bad
news about her cousin.

4. When we fought, my sister treated me with _____ and anger.

5. In many poems, the speaker will often _____ in his or her
unhappiness.

EXERCISE B   Responding to the Selection

On the back of this sheet, use three vocabulary words to write a short paragraph
summarizing one of the sonnets. Be sure to describe all of the speaker's main
ideas.

Vocabulary Development

Of Studies SIR FRANCIS BACON

UNIT 2

Selection Vocabulary

discourse (dis′ kôrs′) *n.* verbal communication in speech or writing
execute (ek′ sə kūt′) *v.* to carry out, to put into effect
sloth (sloth) *n.* laziness
impediment (im ped′ ə mənt) *n.* an obstacle

EXERCISE A   Determining Meaning

For each sentence below, write the selection vocabulary word that completes the sentence.

1. It was Saturday morning, so Paula decided she could indulge her _____ by sleeping late.

2. The fallen tree was an _____ across the hiker's trail.

3. The physics lecturer's clear, energetic _____ was easy to follow.

4. The CEO wondered how many plans he would have to _____ before one worked.

EXERCISE B   Applying Meaning

Additional Vocabulary

rhetoric (ret ər′ ik) *n.* the skill of speaking or writing effectively or persuasively
conference (kon fər əns) *n.* a conversation

Write the additional vocabulary word that answers each question.

1. What might you organize to gather opinions from people? _____

2. Which word refers to the use of language? _____

EXERCISE C   Responding to the Selection

On the back of this sheet, use three vocabulary words to write a summary of Sir Francis Bacon's idea from the selection. Do you agree or disagree with his thoughts?

Vocabulary Development

Sonnet 116 *and* Sonnet 130 WILLIAM SHAKESPEARE

Selection Vocabulary

alteration (ôl′ tə rā′ shən) *n.* change; modification
tempest (tem′ pist) *n.* a violent storm; a violent outburst or disturbance
doom (do͞om) *n.* that which cannot be escaped; death, ruin, or destruction
tread (tred) *v.* to walk or step upon

EXERCISE A   Determining Meaning

For each sentence below, write the selection vocabulary word that belongs in the blank.

1. Sharon said that the violent winds made today's weather more like a

_____ than a regular storm.

2. _____ lightly past the bedroom so that you do not wake the

sleeping baby.

3. Sitting outside of the job interview filled Jackson with a great sense of _____.

4. Arlene decided to buy the dress even though she knew it would need

_____ in order to fit properly.

EXERCISE B   Classifying

Write the vocabulary word that belongs with each group of related words. Use a dictionary for help.

1. change, amendment, adaptation, _____

2. blizzard, hurricane, typhoon, _____

3. destruction, end, fate, _____

4. run, trample, march, _____

EXERCISE C   Responding to the Selection

On the back of this page, use three vocabulary words to write a paragraph describing love.

Vocabulary Development

Fear No More the Heat o' the Sun *and*

Blow, Blow, Thou Winter Wind WILLIAM SHAKESPEARE

Selection Vocabulary

tyrant (tī′ rənt) *n.* a cruel, oppressive ruler; a ruler with unlimited power
censure (sen′ shər) *n.* strong disapproval; condemnation as wrong
keen (kēn) *adj.* having a sharp edge or point
folly (fol′ ē) *n.* foolishness; an irrational and useless undertaking

EXERCISE A   Determining Meaning

For each sentence below, write the selection vocabulary word that belongs in the blank.

1. They knew that to try climbing the mountain was _____, but they did it anyway.

2. The king was a _____, but everyone was afraid of him, and so he continued to rule.

3. I received probation and _____ after pulling the fire alarm at school.

4. The _____ edge of the kitchen counter cut my arm.

EXERCISE B   Practice with Synonyms

Additional Vocabulary

furious (fyoor′ ē əs) *adj.* extremely angry; enraged
worldly (wurld′ lē) *adj.* wise in the ways of the world; sophisticated
physic (fiz′ ik) *n.* medicine

Match each additional vocabulary word with its synonyms (words with nearly the same meanings). Use a dictionary for help.

1. furious   **A.** experienced, savvy, confident

2. worldly   **B.** tonic, medicine, remedy

3. physic   **C.** angry, incensed, enraged

EXERCISE C   Responding to the Selection

On the back of this sheet, use three vocabulary words to write a response to the speaker in one of the poems. What do you think of the speaker's experience? How would you react similarly or differently?

Vocabulary Development

To be, or not to be *from* **Hamlet** *and* **All the world's a stage**
from **As You Like It** *and* **Our revels now are ended**
from **The Tempest** WILLIAM SHAKESPEARE

Selection Vocabulary

calamity (kə lam′ ə tē) *n.* disaster; extreme misfortune
awry (ə rī′) *adj.* wrong; in a faulty way
oblivion (ə bliv′ ē ən) *n.* a state of forgetting
pageant (paj′ ənt) *n.* an elaborately staged drama or spectacular exhibition
infirmity (in fur′ mə tē) *n.* weakness; state of being feeble or unable

EXERCISE A   Determining Meaning

For each sentence below, write the selection vocabulary word that belongs in the blank.

1. Last night I tried to upload a program, but my computer went _____.

2. My sister took first place in the beauty _____ last year.

3. Everything he tried to make was a complete _____!

4. My grandma had to go to the hospital when she had an _____.

5. Some people think he is really smart, but I think he is in a state of _____.

EXERCISE B   Responding to the Selection

On the back of this sheet, use five vocabulary words to paraphrase the contents of one of the speeches. Be sure to address each of the main points from the speech.

Vocabulary Development
Macbeth, Act 1 WILLIAM SHAKESPEARE

UNIT 2

Selection Vocabulary

direful (dīr′ fəl) *adj.* terrible; dreadful
prophetic (prə fet′ ik) *adj.* having the quality of foretelling future events
repentance (ri pent′ əns) *n.* a feeling of sorrow for wrongdoing; remorse
plenteous (plen′ tē əs) *adj.* abundant; fruitful
peerless (pēr′ lis) *adj.* unrivaled; without equal

EXERCISE A   Determining Meaning

For each sentence below, write the selection vocabulary word that best completes the sentence.

1. The harvest was _____ that year.

2. As a soccer player, Jason was a _____ goalie.

3. The team calmly received the _____ news that Jose would be out for the semester.

4. Joseph cleaned the garage as _____ for breaking the window.

5. Just as she left, Brianna uttered those _____ words, "You'll be sorry."

EXERCISE B   Determining Meaning

Additional Vocabulary

deceive (di sēv′) *v.* mislead; cause to believe what is not accurate
vanished (van′ ish əd) *v.* passed out of sight; passed out of existence
nature (nā′ chər) *n.* material world; real aspect of a person or thing

For each sentence below, write the additional vocabulary word that belongs in the blank.

1. Amelia Earhart _____ while trying to fly across the Pacific Ocean.

2. It is the _____ of business to try to make a profit.

3. Children often try to _____ their parents about their misbehavior.

EXERCISE C   Responding to the Selection

On the back of this sheet, use four vocabulary words to write a paragraph describing Macbeth.

Vocabulary Development

Macbeth, Act 2 WILLIAM SHAKESPEARE

Selection Vocabulary

stealthy (stel′ thē) *adj.* secret; sly
surfeited (sur′ fit əd) *adj.* overfed; overcome by excess drinking, eating, etc.
provoke (prə vōk) *v.* to call forth; to stir to action or feeling
scruple (skrōō′ pəl) *n.* a moral or ethical principle that restrains action
predominance (pri dom′ ə nens) *n.* the state of being most important, common or noticeable

---

EXERCISE A   Determining Meaning

For each sentence below, write the vocabulary word that best completes each sentence.

1. Rachel tried to _____ an argument with Megan.

2. Zoe tried to be _____ when she whispered in Riley's ear.

3. Most people are _____ when they eat at the all-you-can-eat buffet.

4. The color yellow has equal _____ with red on the color wheel.

5. Everyone has at least one _____.

EXERCISE B   Practice with Synonyms

Additional Vocabulary

consent (kən sent′) *v.* agree; to give assent
instrument (in′ strə mənt) *n.* implement used in work; device for playing music
business (biz′ nis) *n.* commercial enterprise; occupation; pursuit
thoughts (thôts) *n.* products of thinking; act of thinking
building (bil′ ding) *n.* something that is built; act of construction

Draw a line to connect each additional vocabulary word to its synonym (word with nearly the same meaning). Use a dictionary for help.

1. consent   **A.** structure

2. instrument   **B.** approval

3. business   **C.** musings

4. thoughts   **D.** work

5. building   **E.** device

EXERCISE C   Responding to the Selection

On the back of this sheet, use five vocabulary words to write a paragraph describing the changes in Macbeth.

Vocabulary Development

Macbeth, Act 3 WILLIAM SHAKESPEARE

Selection Vocabulary

indissoluble (in′ di sol′ yə bəl) *adj.* incapable of being broken; permanent
incensed (in senst′) *adj.* enraged; filled with anger
jovial (jō′ vē əl) *adj.* full of good humor; genial and playful
appall (ə pôl) *v.* to fill with horror and shock
amends (ə mendz′) *n.* something done or given to make up for injury, loss, etc.

EXERCISE A   Determining Meaning

For each sentence below, write the selection vocabulary word that belongs in the blank.

1. The insulting remark _____ Carlos.

2. Scary movies _____ some sensitive people.

3. It is not easy to make _____ when you have hurt someone's feelings.

4. The building's foundation was considered _____.

5. During the winter holidays, most people are _____ and can enjoy themselves.

EXERCISE B   Practice with Antonyms

Additional Vocabulary

guide (gīd) *v.* direct the course of; steer; control; supervise training
reckless (rek′ lis) *adj.* heedless; careless; headstrong; rash
absence (ab′ səns) *n.* state of being away; lack; want
resolved (ri zolvd′) *v.* made a firm decision; changed; converted; had a successful conclusion

Draw a line to connect each additional vocabulary word to its antonym, or word with nearly the opposite meaning. Use a dictionary for help.

1. guide   **A.** undetermined

2. reckless   **B.** prudent

3. absence   **C.** presence

4. resolved   **D.** follow

EXERCISE C   Responding to the Selection

On the back of this sheet, use four vocabulary words to describe what you think is going to happen in Act 4 and Act 5.

Vocabulary Development
Macbeth, Act 4 WILLIAM SHAKESPEARE

Selection Vocabulary

pernicious (pər nish′ əs) *adj.* destructive; deadly
exploit (eks′ ploit ; iks ploit′) *n.* bold deed
redress (ri dres′) *v.* to set right; to remedy
avarice (av′ ər is) *n.* greed
pertain (pər tān′) *v.* to be connected to or to have relevance to

EXERCISE A   Determining Meaning

For each sentence below, write the selection vocabulary word that completes the sentence.

1. Winning all of its basketball games was a remarkable _____ for the team.

2. Daniel's _____ attitude was going to destroy him one day.

3. When you right a wrong, you _____ it.

4. Good grades _____ to the amount of work you do for the class.

5. When people are greedy, they are considered to have _____.

EXERCISE B   Practice with Synonyms

Additional Vocabulary

caution (kô′ shən) *n.* close attention to minimize risk; forethought to avoid danger
fate (fāt) *n.* force that predetermines events; events predestined by this force; final outcome; doom
delights (di līts′) *v.* takes or gives joy or pleasure; greatly pleases
market (mär′ kit) *n.* place where goods are sold; store that sells goods; opportunity to buy or sell

Draw a line to connect each additional vocabulary word to its synonym (word with nearly the same meaning). Use a dictionary for help.

1. caution   **A.** charms

2. fate   **B.** destiny

3. delights   **C.** store

4. market   **D.** vigilance

EXERCISE C   Responding to the Selection

On the back of this sheet, use four vocabulary words to write a paragraph describing your favorite part of the drama so far.

Vocabulary Development

Macbeth, Act 5 WILLIAM SHAKESPEARE

Selection Vocabulary

purge (purj) *n.* the process of getting rid of impurities or undesirable elements

antidote (an′ ti dōt′) *n.* a medicine used to counteract the effects of a poison; any counteracting remedy

siege (sēj) *n.* blockade; the surrounding of a fortified place by an opposing army intending to invade it

prowess (prou′ is) *n.* superior ability; skill

usurper (ū surp′ ər) *n.* one who seizes the power, position, or rights of another by force

EXERCISE A Determining Meaning

For each sentence below, write the selection vocabulary word that best completes the sentence.

1. Jim showed his _____ by lifting the weights.

2. The king became a _____ when he dethroned his uncle.

3. Companies often _____ their files to clean out their storage areas.

4. Chicken soup is a good _____ for the common cold.

5. The army laid _____ to the city.

EXERCISE B Determining Meaning

Additional Vocabulary

discovery (dis kuv′ ər ē) *n.* act of discovering; something discovered

revolt (ri vôlt′) *v.* attempt to overthrow authority; rebel; oppose something

recorded (ri kôrd′ əd) *v.* set down for preservation; to register

coward (kou′ ərd) *n.* one who shows ignoble fear in the face of danger

For each sentence below, write the additional vocabulary word that belongs in the blank.

1. José _____ the information in his day planner.

2. The _____ of the planet was an important historical event.

3. When Jake ran away, his friends called him a _____.

4. The _____ of the province was the beginning of a civil war.

EXERCISE C Responding to the Selection

On the back of this sheet, write two paragraphs describing how the predictions of the Apparitions came true. Use three vocabulary words.

UNIT 2

Vocabulary Development

from Genesis *and* Psalm 23 THE KING JAMES VERSION OF THE BIBLE

Selection Vocabulary

abundantly (ə bun′ dənt lē) *adv.* plentifully
replenish (ri plen′ ish) *v.* to refill or make complete again; to add a new supply to
beguile (bi gīl′) *v.* to mislead by trickery; to deceive
enmity (en′ mə tē) *n.* ill will; hostility

EXERCISE A   Determining Meaning

For each sentence below, write the selection vocabulary word that belongs in the blank.

1. My mother taught me never to treat others with _____.

2. Oranges grow _____ throughout the state of Florida.

3. It was Maria's job to _____ the dessert trays as soon as they became empty.

4. The fox tried to _____ the hunter.

EXERCISE B   Practice with Synonyms

Additional Vocabulary

firmament (fur′ mə mənt) *n.* the atmosphere surrounding the earth
dominion (də min′ yən) *n.* authority or power to rule
meat (mēt) *n.* food in general
cleave (klēv) *v.* to cling to; to be faithful to

Write the additional vocabulary word that is a synonym (word with nearly the same meaning) for each word or phrase in bold type.

1. The President of the United States has **power** over the citizens of the U.S. _____

2. I like to look up at the nighttime **sky** and see all the stars. _____

3. Sometimes when I am scared, I **hold on** to my teddy bear. _____

4. Farmers and ranchers bring their **produce and other foods** to a local market to trade and barter for other goods. _____

EXERCISE C   Responding to the Selection

On the back of this sheet, use three vocabulary words to write a paragraph in which you summarize the main points of the selections. Be sure to refer to specific parts of the text in your response.

UNIT 2

Vocabulary Development

Eve's Apology AEMILIA LANYER

Selection Vocabulary

endure (en door′) *v.* to bear; tolerate; put up with
discretion (dis kresh′ ən) *n.* good judgment

EXERCISE A	Determining Meaning

For each sentence below, write the selection vocabulary word that best completes each sentence.

1. You need to use _____ when buying a new car.

2. When I broke my leg, I had to _____ a lot of pain.

EXERCISE B	Classifying

Additional Vocabulary

frame (frām) *v.* to determine
reprove (re proōv′) *v.* to scold or correct, usually gently
stay (stā) *v.* to prevent; stop; halt
breach (brēch) *n.* violation; failure to observe a law or promise

Match each additional vocabulary word with the appropriate group of related words. Use a dictionary for help.

1. frame   **A.** rupture, break, lapse

2. breach   **B.** remain, rest, persevere

3. reprove   **C.** support, surround, hold up

4. stay   **D.** disapprove, critique, censure

EXERCISE C	Responding to the Selection

On the back of this sheet, write a response to Lanyer's piece. Do you agree or disagree with the speaker? Why or why not? Use three vocabulary words.

UNIT 2

Vocabulary Development

Song, A Valediction: Forbidding Mourning, *and*

Death Be Not Proud JOHN DONNE

Selection Vocabulary

jest (jest) *n.* an utterance or act offered humorously or mockingly
refine (ri fīn′) *v.* to free from imperfections; to improve

EXERCISE A   Determining Meaning

For each sentence below, write the selection vocabulary word that best
completes the sentence.

1. In order to _____ his basketball skills, he had to practice every
day.

2. A joke is a statement made in _____.

EXERCISE B   Practice with Synonyms

In the chart below, list three synonyms (words with nearly the same meaning)
for each of the selection vocabulary words. Use a dictionary or thesaurus for
help.

JEST	REFINE

EXERCISE C   Responding to the Selection

Donne used poetry to explore topics that might seem simple, but often turn
out to have unexpected meanings. On the back of this sheet, create a poem
that uses one selection vocabulary word. In your poem, reflect on the hidden
meanings of a simple idea or event.

UNIT 2

Vocabulary Development

Meditation 17 JOHN DONNE

UNIT 2

Selection Vocabulary

congregation (kong′ grə gā′ shən) n. a group of people who gather for religious worship

covetousness (kuv′ it əs nes) n. great desire for something belonging to another

contemplation (kon′ təm plā′ shən) n. careful thought or consideration; meditation

EXERCISE A   Determining Meaning

For each sentence below, write the selection vocabulary word that belongs in the blank.

1. The _____ prayed together.

2. _____ can help people think of solutions to problems.

3. When our friend owns a car that we admire, it is easy to feel _____.

EXERCISE B   Determining Meaning

Addditional Vocabulary

tolls (tôls) v. sounds slowly and at regular intervals

translated (trans lāt′ əd) v. expressed differently

mingled (ming′ gəld) adj. combined without losing traits of each part

affliction (ə flik′ shən) n. pain; misery; suffering

For each sentence below, write the additional vocabulary word that belongs in the blank.

1. My personal suffering and _____ were nothing compared to my parents' hardship.

2. The town clock bell _____ and chimes on each hour.

3. The dancer _____ his ideas into flowing movements.

4. I tasted the _____ flavors of butter, apples, cinnamon, and sugar in the pie.

EXERCISE C   Responding to the Selection

On the back of this sheet, use three vocabulary words to write a paragraph on how a tolling bell was used in Donne's time to announce that someone was dead.

Vocabulary Development

The Constant Lover *and*

Why So Pale and Wan, Fond Lover? SIR JOHN SUCKLING

UNIT 2

Selection Vocabulary

constant (kon′ stənt) *adj.* never stopping, continuous; faithful, steadfast
spite (spīt) *n.* desire to annoy or harm; ill will
prevail (pri vāl′) *v.* to be in general use; succeed

EXERCISE A Determining Meaning

For each sentence below, write the selection vocabulary that belongs in the blank.

1. Franklin raged in a fit of _____, angry about his enemy's insults.

2. Laura will _____ in her defense of her friend.

3. The _____ hammering gave the builder a headache.

EXERCISE B Practice with Antonyms

Additional Vocabulary

mute (mūt) *adj.* not speaking; silent
due (dōo) *adj.* owed; expected; looked for

Select the antonym (word with the opposite meaning) for each word. Use a dictionary for help.

1. mute
  A. quiet   **B.** talkative   **C.** secretive   **D.** inspired

2. due
  A. late   **B.** completed   **C.** honored   **D.** unanticipated

EXERCISE C Responding to the Selection

On the back of the sheet, write a paragraph summarizing the main ideas of one of the poems by Sir John Suckling. Which one can you most easily identify with and why? Use two vocabulary words in your paragraph.

UNIT 2

Vocabulary Development

To Lucasta, Going to the Wars *and*

To Althea, from Prison RICHARD LOVELACE

Selection Vocabulary

chaste (chāst) *adj.* pure; virtuous; modest
inconstancy (in kon′ stən sē) *n.* changeable nature; disloyalty
unconfined (un kən fīnd′) *adj.* not shut in; unrestricted
allaying (ə lā′ ing) *v.* putting at rest; relieving

EXERCISE A   Determining Meaning

For each sentence below, write the selection vocabulary word that belongs in the blank.

1. Allison changed her travel plans repeatedly because of the _____ of her preferences.

2. James was _____ his anxiety about the exam by studying hard.

3. My parents approved of my friendship with Emily because of her _____ remarks to them.

4. The dogs ran down the street, _____ by walls or fences.

EXERCISE B   Practice with Synonyms

Additional Vocabulary

foe (fō) *n.* enemy; opponent
embrace (em brās′) *v.* to take up eagerly
adore (ə dôr′) *v.* to worship with deep love
divine (di vīn′) *adj.* heavenly; supremely good or beautiful

Circle the synonym (word with nearly the same meaning) for each vocabulary word below. Use a dictionary for help.

1. embrace:	accept	reject	acknowledge	ignore
2. divine:	wonderful	guess	natural	famous
3. foe:	idea	force	opponent	folly
4. adore:	consider	pursue	blame	cherish

EXERCISE C   Responding to the Selection

How does Richard Lovelace feel about love? Select either "To Lucasta, Going to the Wars" or "To Althea, from Prison" and look for evidence to support your opinion. Write a paragraph explaining your viewpoint on the back of this sheet. Use three vocabulary words.

Vocabulary Development

To His Coy Mistress ANDREW MARVELL

Selection Vocabulary

hue (hū) *n.* color, shade, or tint
strife (strīf) *n.* unrest or violent conflict

EXERCISE A   Applying Meaning

For each item below, write the selection vocabulary word that answers the question.

1. What would a city torn by civil war have? _____

2. How would you describe a shade of color? _____

EXERCISE B   Responding to the Selection

On the back of this sheet, write one paragraph about a relationship that you have had with a friend. Use three vocabulary words.

UNIT 2

Vocabulary Development

from **Paradise Lost** JOHN MILTON

Selection Vocabulary

transgress (trans gres′) *v.* to break or violate a law; to go beyond a limit
deluge (del′ ūj) *n.* something that overwhelms as if by a flood
discern (di surn′) *v.* to perceive; to detect
myriad (mir ′ ē əd) *n.* a great or countless number
subterranean (sub′ tə rā′ nē ən) *adj.* below the earth's surface; underground

EXERCISE A Determining Meaning

For each sentence below, write the vocabulary word that belongs in the blank.

1. In the darkness it was difficult to _____ the direction of the footpath.

2. We followed a _____ trail under the city.

3. The _____ of water covered the streets in a matter of hours.

4. The shopping mall offered us a _____ of options for buying new school clothes.

5. Even though the rules were clearly laid out, some students chose to _____ them.

EXERCISE B Classifying

Additional Vocabulary

rebellious (ri bel′ yəs) *adj.* behaving or disposed to be like a rebel
horrid (hôr′ id) *adj.* causing aversion or horror; dreadful
wrath (rath) *n.* extreme anger; rage
vengeance (ven′ jəns) *n.* act or instance of inflicting injury in return for an injury or offense received

Write the vocabulary word that best completes each group of related words.
Use a dictionary for help.

1. nasty, unkind, terrible, _____

2. anger, rage, fury, _____

3. disobedient, unruly, defiant, _____

4. revenge, retaliation, repayment, _____

EXERCISE C Responding to the Selection

Milton describes good and evil. On the back of this sheet, use four vocabulary words to write a paragraph about a time you felt torn between good and evil.

Leveled Vocabulary Development, Adapted

Vocabulary Development

from **The Pilgrim's Progress** JOHN BUNYAN

Selection Vocabulary

diverse (dī vurs') *adj.* markedly different
indictment (in dīt' mənt) *n.* a formal accusation
reconciled (rek' ən sil' əd) *adj.* brought to acceptance of

EXERCISE A Determining Meaning

For each sentence below, write the selection vocabulary word that belongs in the blank.

1. After his _____, the criminal was put on trial.

2. The father never became _____ to his son's bright pink hair.

3. The grocery store had a _____ selection of fruit.

EXERCISE B Responding to the Selection

On the back of this page, use three vocabulary words to write a paragraph describing the main events of *The Pilgrim's Progress*.

Copyright © by The McGraw-Hill Companies, Inc.

UNIT 3

Vocabulary Development

On Her Loving Two Equally APHRA BEHN

election Vocabulary

passion (pash' ən) *n.* powerful emotion; love
subdue (səb doo') *v.* to conquer
mourn (môrn) *v.* to show or feel sadness; grieve

A	Determining Meaning

For each sentence below, write the selection vocabulary word that best completes the sentence.

The general tried to _____ the rebel population, but their numbers were too many.

We need time to _____ the loss of our family dog; he was a great pet.

3 Many love poems from different time periods address human _____.

B	Responding to the Selection

On the back of this sheet, use three selection and/or additional vocabulary words to write a paragraph describing the advice you would give to the poem's narrator.

UNIT 3

Vocabulary Development

from **An Essay of Dramatic Poesy** JOHN DRYDEN

election Vocabulary

insipid (in sip′ id) *adj.* lacking interest; dull
bombast (bom′ bast) *n.* pretentious language
esteem (es tēm′) *n.* favorable opinion
superfluous (soo pur′ floo əs) *adj.* beyond what is necessary
monarch (mon′ ərk) *n.* one who rules over a state or territory, usually by
   hereditary right, as a king or queen

A   Determining Meaning

Write the selection vocabulary word that best answers each question.

How could you describe something that is unnecessary? _____

What is respect and liking for a person? _____

3 How could you describe something boring and lifeless? _____

4 What is the ruler of a country? _____

5 What is pretentious language? _____

B   Using Context Clues

Additional Vocabulary

spectacle (spek′ tə kəl) *n.* an eye-catching or dramatic public display
wit (wit) *n.* clever humor
derive (di rīv′) *v.* to take from a specified source
ornamental (ôr′ nə ment′ əl) *adj.* lending grace or beauty
endeavor (en dev′ ər) *v.* to try to achieve or reach

Choose the best meaning for each additional vocabulary word.

In her paper, Charlotte will **derive** her conclusions from many sources.
A write   **B** take   research

His **wit** made him an amusing companion.
A humor   **B** laugh   strangeness

3 Sandra will **endeavor** to climb over the wall, but it looks too high.
A decline   **B** fail   try

4 The play put on in the middle of the square created quite a **spectacle** for
the town.
A interest   **B** disaster   display

5 The **ornamental** picture frame included beautiful carved wood.
A expensive   **B** decorative   old-fashioned

UNIT 3

Vocabulary Development
from **The Diary of Samuel Pepys** SAMUEL PEPYS

election Vocabulary

cavalcade (kav ′ əl kād′) *n.* a ceremonial procession
loath (lōth) *adj.* reluctant; unwilling
quench (kwench) *v.* to put out; to extinguish
malicious (mə lish′ əs) *adj.* deliberately harmful

A   Determining Meaning

For each sentence below, write the selection vocabulary word that belongs in the blank.

After the long bike ride, we drank water to _____ our thirst.

The play ended with an impressive _____ of all of the actors.

3 Even though he's not a _____ person, his acts sometimes hurt people.

4 I was _____ to agree to babysit the night before my exam.

B   Applying Meaning

Additional Vocabulary

ado (ə doo′) *n.* bustling excitement
scaffold (skaf′ əld) *n.* raised platform
magnificent (mag nif′ ə sənt) *adj.* strikingly beautiful or impressive
fling (fling) *v.* to throw forcefully or casually
canopy (kan′ ə pē) *n.* a cloth covering

For each sentence below, write the additional vocabulary word that belongs in the blank.

A _____ was raised to allow the bricklayers to work on the new building.

The hikers found the view from the top of the mountain to be _____.

3 They sat under a _____ to protect them from the sun.

4 When Tyrone saw a bee in his drink, it caused him to _____ the can away.

5 There was much _____ behind the scenes as the actors prepared for their first performance.

Responding to the Selection

On the back of this sheet, use four selection and/or additional vocabulary words to write a paragraph about a festive event.

UNIT 3

Vocabulary Development

A Modest Proposal JONATHAN SWIFT

election Vocabulary

sustenance (sus′ tə nəns) *n*. food
deference (def′ ər əns) *n*. courteous respect
digress (di gres′) *v*. to stray from the main subject

A   Determining Meaning

For each sentence below, write the selection vocabulary word that best completes the sentence.

Famous and powerful people are often treated with great _____.

In winter, it can be hard for animals to find enough _____ to survive.

3 Paul always wanted to _____ when he told a story.

B   Understanding Archaic Usage

Use a dictionary to look up each of the following additional vocabulary words from the selection. Select the definition that is more familiar to you. Then complete the chart by writing the definition in the space provided.

Words	Swift's Definition	Modern Definition
dam (dam)	*n*. mother	
dear (dēr)	*adj*. costly, expensive	
service (sur′ vis)	*v*. to work as a servant	
receipts (ri sēts′)	*n*. recipes	

Responding to the Selection

On the back of this sheet, use three vocabulary words to write a paragraph that summarizes Swift's ideas towards poor people as discussed in this selection.

UNIT 3

Vocabulary Development

from **Gulliver's Travels** JONATHAN SWIFT

election Vocabulary

conjecture (kən jek′ chər) *v.* to guess
magnitude (mag′ nə to͞od) *n.* greatness of size or extent

A	Determining Meaning

For each sentence below, write the selection vocabulary word that best completes the sentence.

The Sears Tower is a building of immense _____.

If you don't know the right answer, you can _____ and see if you are correct.

B	Practice with Synonyms

Additional Vocabulary

apprehend (ap′ ri hend′) *v.* to seize or capture someone
fortnight (fôrt′ nīt) *n.* two weeks
avarice (av′ ər is) *n.* desire for wealth or possessions; greed

Write the vocabulary word that fits in the blank in the sentence and is a synonym for the word or phrase in bold type.

The evil giant counted his gold coins each night, full of **greed** and _____.

Each police officer who worked on the case wanted to _____ and **capture** the suspect.

3 I will be traveling through the country for a _____, so I'll return in **two weeks**.

	Responding to the Selection

On the back of this sheet, use two selection and/or additional vocabulary words to describe your favorite part of the excerpt. Why do you like this?

Vocabulary Development

Epigrams *and from* An Essay on Man ALEXANDER POPE

election Vocabulary

commend (kə mend′) *v.* to praise, give approval
discord (dis′ kôrd) *v.* lack of agreement or harmony
disabuse (dis′ ə būz′) *v.* to free from a misconception

A   Applying Meaning

Write the selection vocabulary word that belongs in the blank.

Maria tried to _____ her teacher of the idea that she was involved in the fight.

Hassan wanted to _____ the firefighter for saving his family's house from burning down.

3 Everyone in the cafeteria was talking at once, and the _____ filled Patrick's ears.

B   Applying Meaning

Additional Vocabulary

skeptic (skep′ tik) *n.* one who habitually doubts
stoic (stō′ ik) *n.* someone who seems unaffected by pain or pleasure
err (er) *v.* to do something wrong, make a mistake
prey (prā) *n.* an animal hunted or killed for food; victim

Write the vocabulary word that answers each question.

Which word is a synonym for *mistake*? _____

Which word might describe someone who is hard to convince? _____

3 Which word is an antonym for *predator*? _____

4 Which word is another word for someone who shows little emotion? _____

Responding to the Selection

On the back of this sheet, use three selection and/or additional vocabulary words to write a paragraph in which you agree or disagree with Pope's main idea. Why do you agree or disagree with the author?

UNIT 3

Vocabulary Development
from **The Rape of the Lock** ALEXANDER POPE

election Vocabulary

stratagem (strat′ ə jəm) *n.* a deception; a military tactic designed to surprise an enemy

confound (kən found′) *v.* to confuse, defeat, or overthrow

A   Determining Meaning

For each sentence below, write the selection vocabulary word that belongs in the blank.

The military generals tried to _____ their enemies.

The _____ the army used is famous in history.

B   Applying Meaning

Additional Vocabulary

sprite (sprit) *n.* an elf-like being
foe (fō) *n.* an enemy
vow (vou) *n.* an important promise
inscribe (in skrīb′) *v.* to write or engrave
rash (rash) *adj.* foolish or reckless

Write the additional vocabulary word that best completes the sentence.

Stacy made a _____ to do her homework every day as soon as she got home.

Paul wondered how much it would cost to _____ Lisa's initials on the silver locket.

3 Even though his father thought it was _____, Abdul decided to buy the convertible.

4 After reading many fairy tales, Harriet had always wanted to meet a _____.

5 Mark hoped that he would never have a _____ whom he would have to fight.

Responding to the Selection

On the back of this sheet, use three vocabulary words to summarize the events of Pope's poem.

Vocabulary Development

Letter to Her Daughter LADY MARY WORTLEY MONTAGU

election Vocabulary

edifice (ed′ ə fis) *n.* a building, especially a large one
diversion (di vur′ zhən) *n.* an amusement; an entertainment
inveterate (in vet′ ər it) *adj.* firmly established; deep-rooted
elate (ī lāt′) *v.* to make happy

A Determining Meaning

For each item, write the selection vocabulary word that answers the question.

What do you call a pleasant distraction? _____

What does an uplifting movie do to your mood? _____

3 What would you call a colossal tower sitting on a hill? _____

4 How might you describe a tradition that has lasted for centuries? _____

B Classifying

Write the selection vocabulary word that best completes each group of related words. Use a dictionary if you need help.

usual, fixed, routine, _____

delight, thrill, excite, _____

3 palace, castle, fortress, _____

4 movie, card game, party, _____

Responding to the Selection

Imagine you have a daughter or a son. On the back of this sheet, use two vocabulary words to write a paragraph describing the advice you would give your child.

Vocabulary Development

from **The Spectator** JOSEPH ADDISON and SIR RICHARD STEELE

election Vocabulary

complaisance (kəm plā′ səns) *n.* a willingness to please, be gracious or be courteous

negligence (neg′ li jəns) *n.* an air of careless ease or casualness

irrational (ī rash′ ən əl) *adj.* lacking reason; ill-advised

A   Determining Meaning

Write the selection vocabulary word that best completes each sentence.

A dangerously laid-back person likely exhibits _____.

It would be _____ to let one's pet dogs out of the house during a terrible thunderstorm.

3 Chris demonstrates his _____ by doing every little thing that Ulie asks him to do.

B   Applying Meaning

Write the vocabulary word that answers each question.

Which word can describe someone who acts strangely? _____

Which word is a synonym for acting irresponsibly? _____

3 How might you describe the act of being extremely polite? _____

Responding to the Selection

Pretend that you are either Sir Roger de Coverley or a devoted reader of *The Spectator*. Decide whether you agree with Steele's points. On the back of this sheet, use two vocabulary words to write a response to Steele's article about Sir Roger.

UNIT 3

Vocabulary Development

from **A Journal of the Plague Year** DANIEL DEFOE

election Vocabulary

confining (kən fīn' ing) *adj*. restricting; limiting
oppressed (ə presd') *adj*. burdened; weighed down
defy (di fī') *v*. to resist; to refuse to cooperate with
prodigious (prə dij' əs) *adj*. great in size, number or degree; enormous

A   Determining Meaning

For each item, write the selection vocabulary word that answers the question.

What does a country do when it revolts against a corrupt government? _____

How might you describe being inside a closet with the door closed? _____

3 How would you describe a large sum of money? _____

4 How might you describe someone carrying a bag of rocks on his back? _____

B   Classifying

Write the selection vocabulary word that best completes each group of related words. Use a dictionary if you need help.

disheartened, despondent, broken, _____

huge, immense, outstanding, _____

3 binding, strict, restrictive, _____

4 revolt, mutiny, rebel, _____

Responding to the Selection

On the back of this sheet, use two vocabulary words to write a paragraph comparing and contrasting Defoe's narrative to another piece of historical fiction that you have read.

Vocabulary Development

from A Dictionary of the English Language *and*

Letter to Lord Chesterfield SAMUEL JOHNSON

election Vocabulary

vigilance (vij′ə ləns) *n.* careful watchfulness
intuitive (in tōō′ ə tiv) *adj.* known or perceived without deliberate thought
immutability (ī mū′ tə bil′ ə tē) *n.* unchangeability; permanence
aggregated (ag′ rə gāt′ əd) *adj.* collected; gathered into a whole
exultation (eg′ zul tā′ shən) *n.* joy; elation

A   Determining Meaning

Write the selection vocabulary word that best completes each sentence.

After we gathered responses from each student, we put the
_____ data into a computer program.

She had such an _____ kindness about her; without effort, she
was always friendly.

3 We need _____ to stay safe when walking through unfamiliar
neighborhoods.

4 He shouted with _____ when he won the school debate.

5 The strong stone buildings on campus gave the place a feeling of _____.

B   Classifying

Additional Vocabulary

longevity (lon jev′ ə tē) *n.* long life
obscurities (əb skyoor′ ə tēs) *n.* things that are unclear, hidden, dark, or not
  clearly expressed
syntax (sin′ taks) *n.* the way in which words are put together to form a
  sentence

Write the vocabulary word that best completes each group of related words.
Use a dictionary if you need help.

rules of language, grammar, sentence structure, _____

3 long life, permanence, durability, _____

4 mysteries, shadow, fogs, _____

Applying Meaning

On the back of this sheet, write a list of your favorite words. Then, use three
vocabulary words to write a paragraph explaining why you chose the words on
your list.

Vocabulary Development

from **The Life of Samuel Johnson** JAMES BOSWELL

election Vocabulary

veneration (ven′ ə rā′ shən) *n.* deep respect or reverence
zealous (zel′ əs) *adj.* filled with intense, enthusiastic devotion
impetuous (im pech′ o͞o əs) *adj.* characterized by rushing headlong into
   things; impulsive
precept (prē′ sept) *n.* a rule intended as a guide for conduct or action
ingenuity (in′ jəno͞o′ ə tē) *n.* cleverness; inventiveness

A	**Determining Meaning**

Write the vocabulary word that best completes each sentence.

He was excited and _____ about the new school policy on free
periods.

We need to follow the department's _____ when deciding on
our future program.

3 The group used creativity and _____ in deciding on its plan.

4 Each decision was made with respect and _____ for our school's
reputation.

5 Although it would have been easy to be _____, we decided to
take our time.

B	**Applying Meaning**

Additional Vocabulary

scoundrel (skoun′drel) *n.* a villain
disposition (dis′ pə zish′ ən) *n.* one's usual mood; temperament
conviction (kən vik′ shən) *n.* a fixed or strong belief

Write the additional vocabulary word that best completes each sentence.

His reputation as a clever and aggressive _____ rapidly spread
around the neighborhood.

My dog's _____ is gentle and friendly.

3 Mary stated with absolute _____ that she wanted to be a
teacher someday.

	Responding to the Selection

On the back of this sheet, use three vocabulary words to prepare a list of at least
five interview questions that you would like to ask Boswell. Use what you have
learned in the story to formulate your questions.

UNIT 3

Vocabulary Development

Elegy Written in a Country Churchyard THOMAS GRAY

election Vocabulary

pomp (pomp) *n.* splendid or dignified display

inevitable (i nev' ə tə bəl) *adj.* incapable of being avoided or prevented; certain

genial (jēn' yəl) *adj.* giving warmth and comfort; pleasant or cheerful

uncouth (un kōōth') *adj.* crude; lacking polish, culture, or refinement

kindred (kin' drid) *adj.* like; allied; similar

A	Determining Meaning

Write the selection vocabulary word that best completes each sentence.

The _____ of the concert was heightened by the band members' tailored suits and synchronized dance steps.

The friendly and talkative woman was quite _____.

3 In the morning, the piercing sound of my alarm clock is _____.

4 The _____ diner snarled at the waiter when he forgot one of the appetizers.

5 The two imaginative young children were true _____ spirits.

B	Practice with Synonyms

Draw a line between each vocabulary word and its synonym, or word with nearly the same meaning. Use a dictionary if you need help.

inevitable	**A**	cordial
uncouth	**B**	coarse
3 genial		unavoidable
4 kindred	**D**	resembling

Responding to the Selection

On the back of this sheet, write a one-paragraph response to the imagery used in "Elegy Written in a Country Churchyard." Use at least three of the selection vocabulary words.

UNIT 4

Vocabulary Development

John Anderson, My Jo *and* To a Mouse *and* Auld Lang Syne

ROBERT BURNS

election Vocabulary

dominion (də min′ yən) *n*. control or the exercise of control
bleak (blēk) *adj*. cold, harsh, raw
foresight (fôr′ sīt′) *n*. preparation or concern for the future

A Determining Meaning

Write the selection vocabulary word that best completes each sentence.

I looked through the bus window at the _____ landscape of gray skies and dead leaves.

Jean wished she had had the _____ to know how difficult her new job would be.

3 Under the king's _____, the kingdom grew and prospered.

B Classifying

Write the word that does not belong in each group. Use a dictionary if you need help.

dominion, rule, helplessness, authority _____

foresight, hindsight, forethought, prescience _____

3 bleak, unwelcome, dreary, appreciative _____

Responding to the Selection

On the back of this sheet, write a personal response to Robert Burns's poetry. In your response, comment on the feelings inspired by the poems. Include two of the selection vocabulary words in your response.

UNIT 4

Vocabulary Development

from **A Vindication of the Rights of Woman** MARY WOLLSTONECRAFT

election Vocabulary

indignation (in′ dig nā′ shən) *n.* anger aroused by something unjust or mean
rational (rash′ ən əl) *adj.* able to reason; sensible
faculty (fak′ əl tē) *n.* capacity of the mind; ability; aptitude
congenial (kən jēn′ yəl) *adj.* compatible; agreeable
condescend (kon′ di send′) *v.* to lower oneself

A   Determining Meaning

Write the selection vocabulary word that best completes each sentence.

When Jake's friends were rude and offensive to him, he did not _____ to join them for lunch.

On Harriet's ninety-fifth birthday, her mental _____ was as sharp as ever.

3 I felt strong _____ when the unqualified candidate won the election.

4 Tyler and Sandy get along well; they are a _____ pair.

5 The aliens looked like stones, but they were _____ beings.

B   Practice with Antonyms

Draw a line between each vocabulary word and its antonym, or word with nearly the opposite meaning. Use a dictionary if you need help.

rational	**A** hostile	
congenial	**B** inability	
3 faculty	peacefulness	
4 indignation	**D** insane	

Responding to the Selection

On the back of this sheet, write a paragraph summarizing one of the selections from *A Vindication of the Rights of Woman*. Use at least three of the selection vocabulary words.

UNIT 4

Vocabulary Development
from **The Diary of Fanny Burney** FANNY BURNEY

election Vocabulary

profound (prə found′) *adj.* characterized by deep understanding or insight
zenith (zē′ nith) *n.* a peak; the greatest point
sanguine (sang′gwin) *adj.* confident; optimistic
droll (drōl) *adj.* amusingly odd
confound (kən found′) *v.* to confuse; to bewilder

A	Determining Meaning

Write the selection vocabulary word that best completes each sentence.

The philosophy professor's _____ remarks consistently demonstrate his deep understanding of life.

Believe me, the riddle will _____ you—it has been puzzling me for hours.

3 I reached the highest point in my life, my _____, when I won the contest.

4 The _____ clown made the children giggle with his silent impressions of various animals.

5 A _____ speaker, she always gives hopeful speeches.

B	Applying Meaning

Write the vocabulary word that answers each question.

Jonathan had high hopes for the future. He was positive and self-assured.
How could you describe Jonathan? _____

The book had a deep and thoughtful message that spoke to me. It made me think about life differently.
How could you describe the book's message? _____

3 The performance was unusual but hysterical. The acrobats did a series of flips while dressed up in banana costumes.
How could you describe the performance? _____

Responding to the Selection

On a separate sheet of paper, write a diary entry about a significant day in your life. Use at least two selection vocabulary terms in your entry.

UNIT 4

Vocabulary Development
from **Pride and Prejudice** JANE AUSTEN

election Vocabulary

hypocritical (hip′ ə krit′ ə kəl) *adj.* describes a person who says one thing but does the opposite

acquaintance (ə kwānt′ əns) *n.* a person one is familiar with

emphatic (em fat′ ik) *adj.* with strong emphasis

A   Determining Meaning

Write the selection vocabulary word that best completes each sentence.

Her _____ was acting quite strangely at the party.

His behavior was so _____! He said we shouldn't eat candy, and yet he had a whole stash of candy in his car!

3 Laura was quite _____ about her point at the meeting. She wouldn't take "no" for an answer.

B   Applying Meaning

Additional Vocabulary

universally (ū′ nə vur′ sə lē) *adj.* understood by everyone

disposition (dis′ pə zish′ ən) *n.* somebody's usual mood or temperament

vexed (vekst) *adj.* irritated; provoked

conceited (kən sē′ tid) *adj.* too proud; having or showing an excessively high opinion of one's own qualities and abilities

Write the vocabulary word that could replace the word or phrase in bold type.

He was quite **annoyed** that his sister got to use the car when he had asked for it first. _____

It is **generally** believed that human actions are the biggest threat to the environment. _____

3 Grumpiness and moodiness are just part of her **character.** _____

4 We all agree that Jackie's **arrogant and snobbish** attitude is the source of all her problems. _____

Responding to the Selection

On the back of this sheet, write a paragraph describing the character in the selection that you find the most appealing or interesting. Use at least two selection and/or additional vocabulary words.

UNIT 4

Vocabulary Development

The World is Too Much with Us *and* It Is a Beauteous Evening,
Calm and Free *and* My Heart Leaps Up *and* Composed Upon
Westminster Bridge, September 3, 1802 WILLIAM WORDSWORTH

election Vocabulary

sordid (sôr′ did) *adj.* filthy; selfish; greedy; mean
piety (pī′ e tē) *n.* devoutness; reverence

A   Determining Meaning

Write the selection vocabulary word that best completes each sentence.

Joey was well known for his _____ and devotion to his family.

Everyone knew about the _____ business transaction and many
were anxious to talk about it.

B   Classifying

Additional Vocabulary

eternal (ī turn′ əl) *adj.* without beginning or end; existing outside of time
outworn (out′ wôrn′) *adj.* no longer useable; not practical
majesty (maj′ is tē) *n.* supreme authority; royalty

Write the vocabulary word that best completes each group of related words.
Use a dictionary if you need help.

grandeur, nobility, monarch, _____

ageless, continual, unfading, immortal, _____

3 obsolete, old-fashioned, aged, outdated, _____

Responding to the Selection

On the back of this sheet, write a paragraph that describes how you view
nature and the outdoors by using at least two of the selection and/or additional
vocabulary words.

UNIT 4

Vocabulary Development

Lines Composed a Few Miles Above Tintern Abbey WILLIAM WORDSWORTH

election Vocabulary

secluded (si klood' ed) *adj.* shut off from others; undisturbed
repose (ri poz') *v.* lie at rest; rest from work or toil

A   **Determining Meaning**

Write the selection vocabulary word that best completes each sentence.

Each weekend they would spend time in _____ and then return
to work Monday.

She was not worried about being _____ because she liked
spending time alone.

B   **Determining Meaning**

Use a dictionary to find the definition of each additional vocabulary word.
Write the definition in the space provided. Then, on a separate sheet of paper,
write a paragraph about nature. In your paragraph, use at least two additional
vocabulary words.

Word	Definition
inland (in' land')	
plots (plots)	
vagrant (vā' grənt)	
genial (jēn'yəl)	
hermit (hur' mit)	

Responding to the Selection

On the back of this sheet, write one paragraph describing the meaning of this
poem. Use at least two of the selection and/or additional vocabulary words.

UNIT 4

Vocabulary Development

The Rime of the Ancient Mariner SAMUEL TAYLOR COLERIDGE

election Vocabulary

dismal (diz′ məl) *adj.* dark and gloomy
penance (pen′ əns) *n.* an act of self-punishment to show repentance for a sin
impart (im pärt′) *v.* to give; donate

A	Determining Meaning

Write the selection vocabulary word that best completes each sentence.

The teacher always tries to _____ nuggets of wisdom to his students.

I completed my _____ by giving some of my favorite things away.

3 Cooper began to shudder as he approached the _____ castle.

B	Practice with Synonyms

Draw a line between each vocabulary word and its synonyms, or words with nearly the same meanings. Use a dictionary if you need help.

dismal   **A** dole, distribute, convey

penance   **B** sad, depressed, weepy

3 impart   atone, repent, remorse

	Responding to the Selection

On the back of this sheet, write a personal response to "The Rime of the Ancient Mariner." How did it make you feel? What images came to mind as you were reading? Use at least two of the selection vocabulary words.

UNIT 4

Vocabulary Development

from The Introduction to Frankenstein MARY SHELLEY

election Vocabulary

incite (in sīt′) *v.* to urge or provoke
illustrious (ī lus′ trē əs) *adj.* famous and distinguished
relinquish (ri ling′ kwish) *v.* to give up; to put aside; to abandon
acute (ə kūt′) *adj.* sharp; intense
transient (tran′ shənt) *adj.* lasting only a brief time; temporary

A   Determining Meaning

Write the selection vocabulary word that best completes each sentence.

The queen did not wish to _____ power, but she knew it was time.

The pain in his leg was _____, and he had to be taken to the hospital immediately.

3 The _____ artist was honored for his great contribution to art.

4 Joseph knew that if he cut in front of the line, he would probably _____ a riot.

5 The summer was as _____ as the rain this year, both seemed to last only a few moments.

B   Applying Meaning

For each sentence below, underline the best ending.

Illustrious people are known by
A hardly anyone.   **B** many people.   only a few people.

Something described as **transient** could be
A a scar.   **B** a boulder.   a fireworks display.

Responding to the Selection

Imagine that you are part of the group including Lord Byron and Mary Shelley that is described in the selection from *Frankenstein*. On the back of this sheet, write a paragraph describing a spooky story you would like to write. Use at least two of the selection vocabulary words.

UNIT 4

Vocabulary Development

She Walks in Beauty *and*
from Childe Harold's Pilgrimage GEORGE GORDON, LORD BYRON

election Vocabulary

spurn (spurn) *v.* to reject or drive off
arbiter (är′ bə tər) *n.* a judge
mar (mär) *v.* to spoil or damage

A Determining Meaning

Write the selection vocabulary word that best completes each sentence.

Will you _____ his request to be his date for the homecoming dance, or will you accept it?

Be careful not to _____ the table with your tools.

3 A(n) _____ was hired to settle the dispute between the two neighbors.

B Classifying

Write the selection vocabulary word that best completes the group of words listed below.

harm, injure, hurt, _____

referee, umpire, mediator, _____

3 refuse, decline, scorn, _____

Responding to the Selection

Using two of the selection vocabulary words, write four sentences describing something you like about the natural world. Use the back of this sheet.

UNIT 4

Vocabulary Development

Ozymandias, Ode to the West Wind, *and* To a Skylark

PERCY BYSSHE SHELLEY

election Vocabulary

dirge (durj) *n.* a song sung in grief; a mournful hymn
cleave (klēv) *v.* to tear or rip; to split something apart
tumult (tōō′ məlt) *n.* disorder; an uproar
satiety (sə tī′ ə tē) *n.* a feeling of wariness or even dislike of something caused
  by satisfying an appetite or desire for it in excess

A   Determining Meaning

Write the selection vocabulary word that best completes each sentence.

I had the feeling of _____ after my second helping of turkey and
mashed potatoes last Thanksgiving.

I used the knife to _____ the apple into two pieces.

3 We sang a _____ at my neighbor's funeral.

4 _____ rocked the organization after the president unexpectedly
resigned.

B   Practice with Synonyms

Draw a line between each vocabulary word and its synonyms, or words with
nearly the same meanings. Use a dictionary if you need help.

dirge	**A** fullness, satisfaction
cleave	**B** hymn, lament
3 tumult	slice, slash
4 satiety	**D** commotion, mayhem

Responding to the Selections

On the back of this sheet, use two selection vocabulary words to write a
summary of one of Shelley's poems.

UNIT 4

Vocabulary Development
La Belle Dame sans Merci *and*

When I Have Fears That I May Cease to Be JOHN KEATS

election Vocabulary

loitering (loi′ tər ing) *v.* standing or lingering idly about a place
glean (glēn) *v.* to collect slowly and carefully; to gather crops left on a field after reaping
teeming (tēm′ ing) *adj.* full; at the point of overflowing

A	**Determining Meaning**

Write the selection vocabulary word that best completes each sentence.

As you read each article, try to _____ the information you will need in order to write your essay.

The restaurant was _____ with people, so we went to the ice cream shop instead.

3 "Stop _____ in the hallways," the hall monitor said to the students. "Get to class!"

B	**Applying Meaning**

Additional Vocabulary

withered (with′ ərd) *v.* dried up; shriveled
anguish (ang′ gwish) *n.* agonizing physical or mental pain; torment
relish (rel′ ish) *n.* strong appreciation or liking

Using the definitions above, fill in the correct word in the space provided.

The roses _____ just a week after Valentine's Day, so Jena pressed them in her scrapbook as a memento.

Jonathan's _____ for video games keeps him up late every night of the week.

3 The _____ Brittany felt when her grandmother passed away was almost too much to bear.

Responding to the Selections

On the back of this sheet, use two vocabulary words in a paragraph that explains which Keats poem you like more and why.

Vocabulary Development

Ode on a Grecian Urn JOHN KEATS

deities (dē′ ə tēs) *n.* gods or goddesses; divinities
desolate (des′ ə lit) *adj.* destitute of inhabitants; deserted

A   Determining Meaning

Write the selection vocabulary word that best completes each sentence.

The _____ city was silent and still.

In ancient myths, _____ often have many human qualities, such as envy or greed.

B   Practice with Synonyms

Additional Vocabulary

urn (urn) *n.* a vase, usually with feet or other type of base
mortals (môrt′ əls) *n.* human beings
grieve (grēv) *v.* to mourn; to feel sorrow

Select the synonym for each additional vocabulary word in italics, and write it on the space provided. Use a dictionary if you need help.

grieve: ignore, forget, welcome, lament: _____

urn: container, figurine, statue, insignia: _____

3 *mortals*: saints, animals, morals, people: _____

Vocabulary Development

To Autumn JOHN KEATS

Selection Vocabulary

conspiring (kən spīr′ ing) *v.* planning or plotting secretly
furrow (fur′ ō) *n.* a long, narrow trench in the ground made by a plow; a rut, groove or wrinkle

EXERCISE A   Determining Meaning

Write the selection vocabulary word that best completes each sentence.

1. The spies were _____ to steal the battle plans.

2. The farmer dug a long _____ to plant the seeds.

EXERCISE B   Applying Meaning

Additional Vocabulary

mellow (mel′ ō) *adj.* ripe; sweet
reaped (rēp′ d) *adj.* harvested; cut (as a grain)
hue (hū) *n.* shade; color

Using the additional vocabulary words above, answer each question on the line provided.

1. Which word might refer to the rosy appearance of the fields? _____

2. Which word describes the fruitfulness of autumn? _____

3. Which word describes what farmers might have done in the field during autumn? _____

EXERCISE C   Responding to the Selection

On the back of this sheet, write a paragraph that summarizes the selection. Use at least two of the selection and additional vocabulary words.

UNIT 4

Name _____ Class _____ Date _____

Vocabulary Development

from **In Memoriam A. H. H.** *and* **Crossing the Bar**
and **Tears, Idle Tears** *from* **The Princess** ALFRED, LORD TENNYSON

Selection Vocabulary

license (lī′ səns) *n.* freedom used irresponsibly
sloth (sloth) *n.* inactivity; laziness
redress (ri dres′) *n.* remedy; relief
diffusive (di fū′ siv) *adj.* spread out or widely scattered
feigned (fānd) *adj.* pretended; imagined

EXERCISE A   Determining Meaning

Write the selection vocabulary word that best answers each question.

1. What is a cure? _____

2. What is going too far with freedom? _____

3. How would you describe something that is fake? _____

4. What is being spread widely? _____

5. What is another word for *laziness*? _____

EXERCISE B   Understanding Analogies

Additional Vocabulary

stagnate (stag′ nāt) *v.* to cease to advance or develop
taint (tānt) *n.* a contaminating mark or influence
idle (id′ el) *adj.* having no basis or reason
ghastly (gast′ lē) *adj.* terrifyingly horrible to the senses

Choose the word that best completes each analogy.

1. Taint is to **contamination** as **injury** is to _____.
  A. stain   **B.** mark   **C.** wound

2. Stagnate is to **develop** as **hope** is to _____.
  A. despair   **B.** love   **C.** advancement

3. Ghastly is to **ghost** as **young** is to _____.
  A. child   **B.** grandmother   **C.** old

4. Idle is to **well-founded** as **peace** is to _____.
  A. tranquility   **B.** quiet   **C.** war

EXERCISE C   Responding to the Selection

On the back of this sheet, use four of the vocabulary words to write a paragraph
in which you compare your response to a difficult event with Tennyson's.

Vocabulary Development

Ulysses ALFRED, LORD TENNYSON

Selection Vocabulary

prudence (proo͞d′ əns) *n.* sound judgment; careful management
abide (ə bīd′) *v.* to remain

EXERCISE A | Determining Meaning

Write the selection vocabulary word that best completes each sentence.

1. If we choose to _____ here, there is a risk of flooding from the overflowing river.

2. The teacher acted with _____ when her students needed guidance and advice.

EXERCISE B | Using Context Clues

Additional Vocabulary

dole (dōl) *v.* to give or distribute
hoard (hôrd) *v.* to hide away a supply or fund
vile (vīl) *adj.* disgustingly bad

Use the context of each sentence to determine the meaning of the additional vocabulary word.

1. Kate began to **hoard** a supply of food, afraid that later she would have too little to eat.
A. eat   **B.** store   **C.** protect

2. The teacher began to **dole** out books to each of the students.
A. remain   **B.** hide   **C.** give

3. Simon was not sure what had caused the **vile** brown puddle at the bottom of his refrigerator.
A. foul   **B.** kind   **C.** prudent

EXERCISE C | Responding to the Selection

On the back of this sheet, use three vocabulary words to write a paragraph describing one aspect of Ulysses' journey.

UNIT 5

Vocabulary Development

Pied Beauty *and* Spring and Fall: To a Young Child

GERARD MANLEY HOPKINS

Selection Vocabulary

dappled (dap′ əld) *adj.* marked with spots
fallow (fal′ ō) *adj.* plowed but left unseeded
blight (blīt) *n.* a disease caused by parasites that makes plants and trees
  wither and die

EXERCISE A   Determining Meaning

Write the selection vocabulary word that best completes each sentence.

1. The chestnut _____ killed many trees.

2. The farmer left one field _____ so the soil could rest and
replenish itself.

3. The white egg was _____ with brown.

EXERCISE B   Classifying

Write the vocabulary word that best completes each group of related words.
Use a dictionary if you need help.

1. disease, affliction, malady, _____

2. speckled, spotted, stippled, _____

3. bare, empty, unplanted, _____

EXERCISE C   Responding to the Selection

On the back of this sheet, use two vocabulary words to write a paragraph about
your feelings about spring and fall.

UNIT 5

Vocabulary Development

from **Jane Eyre** CHARLOTTE BRONTË

Selection Vocabulary

vacant (vā′ kənt) *adj.* empty
scrutiny (skro͞ot′ ən ē) *n.* close watch or examination
advocate (ad′ və kāt′) *v.* to support or argue for
retaliation (ri tal′ ē ā′ shən) *n.* getting even with; revenge
subside (səb sīd′) *v.* to give way or end

EXERCISE A   Determining Meaning

Write the selection vocabulary word that best completes each sentence.

1. The boys dumped buckets of snow on their friends in _____ for an earlier snowball attack.

2. As a lawyer, Mrs. Martinez will _____ for the best interests of young people.

3. Samantha calmed down and felt her nervousness _____ once the test began.

4. Unable to find an open shelter, the lost dog slept in a _____ building.

5. Political candidates are often under _____ from the media.

EXERCISE B   Classifying

Additional Vocabulary

grim (grim) *adj.* bleak; severe; forbidding
piety (pī′ ə tē) *n.* goodness; faithfulness
deceit (di sēt′) *n.* dishonesty; trickery

For each of the following groups, identify the word that does **not** belong and write that word on the blank.

1. piety, piousness, pity, holiness _____

2. deceit, wickedness, honesty, theft _____

3. great, grim, dismal, ghastly _____

EXERCISE C   Responding to the Selection

On the back of this sheet, use four vocabulary words to write a paragraph describing Jane Eyre or Mr. Brocklehurst.

UNIT 5

Vocabulary Development

My Last Duchess ROBERT BROWNING

Selection Vocabulary

countenance (koun′ tə nəns) *n.* someone's face

trifling (trī′ fling) *v.* treating someone or something as unimportant; showing a lack of proper respect

munificence (mū nif′ ə səns) *n.* great generosity

EXERCISE A	Determining Meaning

Write the selection vocabulary word that best completes each sentence.

1. She was _____ with the children, treating them as if their ideas were meaningless.

2. His _____ showed his emotions clearly; we knew he was shocked by the news.

3. The president of the manufacturing company was known for his _____, largely because of the generous scholarship fund he sponsored.

EXERCISE B	Applying Meaning

Additional Vocabulary

earnest (ur′ nist) *adj.* serious and intense

courtesy (kur′ tə sē) *n.* respect and consideration for others

rarity (rār′ ə tē) *n.* something that is rare

Write the additional vocabulary word that best completes each sentence.

1. Jed's reputation for _____ earned him much admiration.

2. It is a _____ for a cat to live to be twenty-four.

3. Francesca was very _____ in her pursuit of knowledge.

EXERCISE C	Responding to the Selection

On the back of this sheet, use four vocabulary words to write a paragraph about how you perceive the character of the duchess based on the speaker's description.

UNIT 5

Vocabulary Development

from Oliver Twist CHARLES DICKENS

Selection Vocabulary

demolition (dem′ ə lish′ ən) *n.* the state of being demolished or obliterated
extraordinary (iks trôr′ də ner′ ē) *adj.* very unusual or remarkable
philosophical (fil′ ə sof′ i kəl) *adj.* concerned with the deeper meaning of life
inseparable (in sep′ ər bəl) *adj.* linked so closely that it is almost impossible
  to separate

EXERCISE A Determining Meaning

For each item below, write the selection vocabulary word that answers the question.

1. How would you describe two friends who never leave each other's side? _____

2. How would you describe a person who thinks about the meaning of life? _____

3. What would you call the act of knocking down buildings? _____

4. How would you describe someone who went to college when she was
  fourteen years old? _____

EXERCISE B Classifying

Additional Vocabulary

notion (nō′ shən) *n.* a belief or opinion; impulse
solemn (sol′ əm) *adj.* gloomy; sad
depicted (di pikt′əd) *adj.* represented in a picture
prophetic (prə fet′ ik) *adj.* able to foretell events
apprentice (ə pren′ tis) *n.* a beginner; one who is learning

In each of the following groups, identify the word that does **not** belong and
write that word on the blank.

1. excited, brooding, earnest, solemn _____

2. apprentice, student, expert, learner _____

3. notion, idea, belief, clueless _____

4. drew, illustrated, depicted, spoke _____

5. insensitive, clairvoyant, prophetic, visionary _____

EXERCISE C Responding to the Selection

On the back of this sheet, use five vocabulary words to write a paragraph that
describes a time you have followed a rule, even when doing so was difficult.

UNIT 5

Vocabulary Development

To an Athlete Dying Young *and*

When I Was One-and-Twenty A. E. HOUSMAN

Selection Vocabulary

threshold (thresh' ōld) *n.* doorway; entranceway
fleet (flēt) *adj.* swift; fast
rue (rōō) *v.* to have sorrow; to have remorse

EXERCISE A   Determining Meaning

Write the selection vocabulary word that answers the question.

1. What do you cross as you enter a room? _____

2. What is another word for *regret*? _____

3. How would you describe someone who moves quickly? _____

EXERCISE B   Practice with Synonyms

Choose the correct synonym for the selection vocabulary word used in each sentence.

1. Falling into the creek caused Julie to **rue** hiking.
   A. regret   **B.** celebrate   **C.** hate

2. Evan removed the door in order to paint the **threshold**.
   A. doormat   **B.** window   **C.** doorjamb

3. The cat was too **fleet** for us to catch him.
   A. slow   **B.** old   **C.** quick

EXERCISE C   Responding to the Selection

On the back of this sheet, use two vocabulary words to write a paragraph about a time you have regretted a missed opportunity.

UNIT 5

Vocabulary Development

A Cup of Tea KATHERINE MANSFIELD

Selection Vocabulary

quaint (kwānt) *adj.* pleasingly unusual or odd
odious (ō′ dē əs) *adj.* causing hate, disgust or repugnance
exotic (ig zot′ ik) *adj.* strangely beautiful or fascinating
retort (ri tôrt′) *v.* to reply in a witty, quick or sharp manner

EXERCISE A | Determining Meaning

Write the vocabulary word that best completes each sentence.

1. To Albert, who had grown up in a small town, the city's skyscrapers were
_____ and mysterious.

2. Ms. James filled her cheery apartment with _____ mementos of
her childhood in England.

3. I cannot forgive Michael for his _____ behavior.

4. If we ask her to come to the park with us, she will only _____
that we should have asked her sooner.

EXERCISE B | Practice with Synonyms

Additional Vocabulary

shadowy (shad′ ō ē′) *adj.* faintly perceptible
lacquer (lak′ ər) *n.* a glossy material
frail (frāl) *adj.* not strong; easily broken
flattery (flat′ ər ē) *n.* excessive praise

In each group below, circle the word that is **not** a synonym for each additional
vocabulary word. Use a dictionary if you need help.

1. shadowy: gloomy, vivid, dim, bleak

2. lacquer: polish, veneer, glaze, dullness

3. frail: delicate, sturdy, feeble, insubstantial

4. flattery: applause, compliment, fawning, insult

UNIT 6

Vocabulary Development

Miss Youghal's Sais RUDYARD KIPLING

Selection Vocabulary

unsavory (un sā′ vər ē) *adj.* sinister; morally questionable
compensation (kom′ pən sā′ shən) *n.* something that offsets,
counterbalances or makes up for
suppressing (sə pres′ ing) *v.* prohibiting the publication of or circulation of;
censoring
farce (färs) *n.* a humorous drama in which the situation and characters are
greatly exaggerated

EXERCISE A   Determining Meaning

Write the selection vocabulary word that best completes each sentence.

1. The comedy, a _____, involved twins who were constantly
mistaken for one another.

2. The dictator has been denounced by the leaders of other countries for
_____ free speech.

3. I don't trust Jake. He seems _____ and threatening.

4. Ms. Jones wrote a check to me as _____ for my work in her garden.

EXERCISE B   Determining Meaning

Additional Vocabulary

prying (prī′ ing) *v.* to obtain with effort or difficulty
initiated (ī nish′ ē āt′ ed) *v.* to set going by taking the first step; begin
native (nā′ tive) *adj.* belonging to a particular place by birth
agony (ag′ ə nē) *n.* a violent, intense struggle

Write the additional vocabulary word that best completes each sentence.

1. Ana longed to go home to her _____ Puerto Rico.

2. After hours of _____ and twisting, the plumber was able to pull
the pipe out of the wall.

3. Students _____ a campaign to raise money for the new
gymnasium.

4. The last mile of the marathon was _____ for Marion, who
pulled a muscle in her leg.

EXERCISE C   Responding to the Selection

On the back of this sheet, write a paragraph explaining why Miss Youghal's
parents think Strickland is an undesirable suitor for their daughter. Use two
selection and additional vocabulary words.

UNIT 6

Vocabulary Development
Shooting an Elephant GEORGE ORWELL

Selection Vocabulary

supplant (sə plant′) *v.* to take the place of, often unfairly
despotic (des pot′ ik) *adj.* tyrannical; oppressive
labyrinth (lab′ ə rinth′) *n.* a place containing winding, interconnected
   passages
squalid (skwol′ id) *adj.* dirty or broken down due to poverty or neglect
garish (gār′ ish) *adj.* excessively bright; flashy; gaudy

EXERCISE A | Applying Meaning

Write the selection vocabulary word that answers each question below.

1. Which word refers to a complicated maze or puzzle? _____

2. Which word would you use to describe what an unfair replacement might do? _____

3. Which word describes a cruel or unfair leader? _____

4. Which word could you use to describe a flamboyant outfit? _____

5. Which word might describe a room that has not been cleaned in months? _____

EXERCISE B | Understanding Word Origins

Additional Vocabulary

petty (pet′ ē) *adj.* trivial or insignificant
nimble (nim′ bəl) *adj.* agile or quick-moving
sneering (snēr ing) *adj.* scornful
squeamish (skwē′ mish) *adj.* easily disgusted

Match each additional vocabulary word with its root word.

1. petty   **A.** *snerren*, to chatter or gossip

2. squeamish   **B.** *squaymisch*, easily nauseated, queasy

3. sneering   **C.** *pety*, small

4. nimble   **D.** *numol*, holding much

EXERCISE C | Responding to the Selection

On the back of this sheet or on a separate sheet of paper, write a paragraph
describing how you think you would react to the situation in the story if you
were in the narrator's place. Use two selection and additional vocabulary words.

UNIT 6

Vocabulary Development

Dreamers SIEGFRIED SASSOON

Selection Vocabulary

destiny (des′ tə nē) *n*. fate; what will necessarily happen
feud (fūd) *n*. lengthy, bitter conflict or dispute
fatal (fāt′ əl) *adj*. causing death, destruction or harm

EXERCISE A   Determining Meaning

Write the selection vocabulary word that best completes each sentence.

1. The spiteful _____ between the two families had already gone on for generations.

2. Martin was careful to keep any _____ chemicals away from his children.

3. Sandra believed that a career in theater was her _____.

EXERCISE B   Understanding Analogies

Additional Vocabulary

climax (klī′ maks) *n*. the point of highest dramatic tension
gnaw (nô) *v*. to bite or chew

Choose the word that best completes each analogy. Use a dictionary if you need help.

1. **Gnaw** is to **teeth** as **paint** is to _____.
   A. brush   **B.** painting   **C.** canvas   **D.** can

2. **Climax** is to **peak** as **fight** is to _____.
   A. weapon   **B.** calm   **C.** argument   **D.** angry

UNIT 6

Vocabulary Development

Dulce et Decorum Est WILFRED OWEN

Selection Vocabulary

trudge (trudj) *v.* to walk wearily or laboriously
ecstasy (ek′ stə sē) *n.* a state beyond reason or self-control
vile (vīl) *adj.* repulsive or disgusting

EXERCISE A   Determining Meaning

Write the selection vocabulary word that best completes each sentence.

1. The children had to _____ through the heavy snow to the sledding hill.

2. The ketchup left a _____ stain on the carpet.

3. Andreas was in _____ during the roller coaster ride.

EXERCISE B   Practice with Synonyms

Additional Vocabulary

plunge (plunj) *v.* to be thrown headlong or violently forward
smothering (smuth′ ər ing) *adj.* overcoming through or as if through lack of air

In each group below, circle the word or phrase that is **not** a synonym (word with nearly the same meaning) of each additional vocabulary word. Use a dictionary if you need help.

1. plunge: dive, fall, stand

2. smothering: stifling, helping, suffocating

UNIT 6

Vocabulary Development

Sailing to Byzantium *and* The Second Coming WILLIAM BUTLER YEATS

Selection Vocabulary

artifice (är′ tə fis) *n.* something artificial or constructed rather than natural
anarchy (an′ ər kē) *n.* a complete lack of political order; chaos
conviction (kən vik′ shən) *n.* a strong belief
vex (veks) *v.* disturb; trouble; irritate

EXERCISE A   Determining Meaning

Write the selection vocabulary word that best completes each sentence.

1. Years of unstable government had left the country dangerously close to _____.

2. Laura is already angry; don't _____ her further.

3. In social settings, so much of Cassie's behavior was _____ that she seemed like a different person.

4. David had a firm _____ that people should help those who are less fortunate.

EXERCISE B   Classifying

Additional Vocabulary

gaze (gāz) *n.* to look steadily with fixed attention
fowl (fowl) *n.* a bird of any kind
slouches (slouch′ əs) *v.* to droop or hang carelessly

Write the vocabulary word that best completes each group of related words. Use a dictionary if you need help.

1. chicken, duck, goose, feathers, _____

2. sags, wilts, flops, hangs, _____

3. stare, look, gape, gawk, _____

EXERCISE C   Responding to the Selection

"Sailing to Byzantium" is a poem about escape. Write a paragraph using two selection vocabulary words about where you go to escape or relax.

UNIT 6

Vocabulary Development

Preludes T. S. ELIOT

Selection Vocabulary

constituted (kon′ stə tōōt′ əd) *v.* made up; formed; comprised
infinitely (in′ fə nit lē) *adv.* boundlessly; endlessly

EXERCISE A | Determining Meaning

Write the selection vocabulary word that best completes each sentence.

1. The vast ocean seemed to stretch out _____ in all directions.

2. The class was _____ of a variety of students from all
backgrounds, united by their interest in history.

EXERCISE B | Applying Meaning

Additional Vocabulary

withered (with′ ərd) *v.* dried up or shriveled
dingy (din′ jē) *adj.* dirty or discolored
grimy (grī′ mē) *adj.* covered in thick dirt

Write the additional vocabulary word that could replace the word or phrase in
bold type in each sentence.

1. Eric's boots were **messy and muddy** when he got home from the hike. _____

2. Two weeks without water had left my garden **wilted and dry.** _____

3. The old newspapers had a **faded, yellowish** tint. _____

EXERCISE C | Responding to the Selection

On the back of this sheet or on a separate sheet of paper, write a paragraph
describing your feelings about the poem. Use two of the selection and
additional vocabulary words.

Vocabulary Development

The Rocking-Horse Winner D. H. LAWRENCE

Selection Vocabulary

parry (par′ ē) *v.* to respond, as to a question or argument, by warding off or diverting

obstinately (ob′ stə nit lē) *adv.* in a manner not yielding to argument, persuasion, or reason; inflexibly

reiterate (rē it′ ə rāt′) *v.* to say or do again; to repeat

emancipate (ī man′ sə pāt′) *v.* to free; to liberate

EXERCISE A Determining Meaning

Write the selection vocabulary word that best completes each sentence.

1. When nobody answered, Ellen had to _____ her question.

2. Leah _____ refused to consider her sister's suggestion.

3. The new government promised to _____ the peasants, who had suffered for decades under a brutal dictatorship.

4. The candidate used a clever remark to _____ the journalist's probing question.

EXERCISE B Responding to the Selection

On the back of this sheet or on a separate sheet of paper, write four sentences explaining why you think money was so important to Paul's family. Use two selection or additional vocabulary words.

Vocabulary Development

Araby JAMES JOYCE

Selection Vocabulary

converge (kən verj′) *v.* to come together in a common interest or conclusion; to center

impinge (im pinj′) *v.* to strike or dash; to collide

amiability (ā mē ə bil′ i tē) *n.* kindliness, friendliness

EXERCISE A   Determining Meaning

Write the vocabulary word that best completes each sentence.

1. Thanks to Joshua's _____, I quickly felt comfortable in the new classroom.

2. I know you and Jane like different things, but your interests must _____ somewhere.

3. Marisa was hesitant to practice parking for fear that her car would _____ on the one behind her.

EXERCISE B   Applying Meaning

For each item, write the selection vocabulary word that answers the question.

1. What is another word for *likeability*? _____

2. What do two cars do in an accident? _____

3. What do lines do when they meet? _____

EXERCISE C   Responding to the Selection

On the back of this sheet or on a separate sheet of paper, write a paragraph describing an epiphany or minor realization you have experienced. Use two of the selection vocabulary words.

UNIT 6

Vocabulary Development
from **A Room of One's Own** VIRGINIA WOOLF

Selection Vocabulary

guffaw (gu fô′) *v.* to laugh loudly and boisterously
thwart (thwôrt) *v.* to prevent from doing or achieving something
hinder (hin′ dər) *v.* to make difficult the progress of; to hold back
dilemma (di lem′ ə) *n.* a situation requiring a choice between equal
  alternatives
morbid (môr′ bid) *adj.* overly sensitive to death and decay; not cheerful or
  wholesome

EXERCISE A   Applying Meaning

For each item, write the selection vocabulary word that answers the question.

1. What does rain do when it slows cars down on the freeway? _____

2. How might you describe a horror movie? _____

3. How might you react to something hilarious? _____

4. What does a hero do when he prevents a villain's evil scheme? _____

5. What are you faced with when you have to choose the lesser of two evils? _____

EXERCISE B   Practice with Synonyms

Draw a line between each vocabulary word and its synonyms, or words with
nearly the same meanings. Use a dictionary if you need help.

1. dilemma   **A.** problem, quandary, choice

2. thwart   **B.** laugh, roar

3. guffaw   **C.** stop, prevent, halt

4. morbid   **D.** deathly, dour, gruesome

EXERCISE C   Responding to the Selection

On the back of this sheet or on a separate sheet of paper, write a paragraph
describing your feelings about Virginia Woolf's role in the battle for women's
rights. Use two of the selection vocabulary words.

UNIT 6

Vocabulary Development
from Mrs. Dalloway VIRGINIA WOOLF

Selection Vocabulary

solemn (sol′ əm) *adj.* serious; somber
presumably (pri zoo′ mə blē′) *adv.* by reasonable assumption
ailment (āl′ ment) *n.* sickness or affliction
perpetual (par pech′ oo əl) *adj.* constantly occurring
cordial (kôr′ jəl) *adj.* personable and likable

EXERCISE A   Determining Meaning

Write the selection vocabulary word that best completes each sentence.

1. Cassie's _____ turned out to be the flu.

2. It was a relief to get away from the _____, formal atmosphere of the funeral.

3. The unmannerly child needs to learn how to be more _____.

4. _____, we can expect this experiment to yield similar results.

5. The temporary building is still being used because of the _____ construction on the new one.

EXERCISE B   Classifying

Additional Vocabulary

bellow (bel′ ō) *v.* to make a loud, hollow sound; to cry out in a loud, deep voice
dejected (di jek′ tid) *v.* low in spirits, disheartened, depressed
vitality (vi tāl′ ə tē) *n.* mental or physical vigor or energy

Write the vocabulary word that best completes each group of related words. Use a dictionary if you need help.

1. sad, downcast, glum, _____

2. life, spirit, strength, _____

3. yell, roar, shout, _____

EXERCISE C   Responding to the Selection

On the back of this sheet or on a separate sheet of paper, write a paragraph describing what you think of Mrs. Dalloway. Use two of the selection and additional vocabulary words.

UNIT 6

Vocabulary Development

Be Ye Men of Valor WINSTON CHURCHILL

Selection Vocabulary

ravage (rav′ ij) *v.* to lay waste to; to destroy
grapple (grap′ əl) *v.* to attempt to deal with; to struggle
imperious (im pēr′ ē əs) *adj.* imperative; urgent
indomitable (in dom′ ə tə bəl) *adj.* incapable of being subdued or overcome

EXERCISE A   Determining Meaning

Write the selection vocabulary word that best completes each sentence.

1. The two wrestlers approached each other and began to _____.

2. "Don't touch that wire!" cried Manny in an _____ voice.

3. Scientists predict that, over time, acid rain will corrode and _____ the statue.

4. The army was small, but the soldiers maintained courage thanks to their fearless, _____ captain.

EXERCISE B   Classifying

Additional Vocabulary

quarreled (kwôr′ əld) *v.* to disagree; differ
barbarism (bär′ bə riz′ əm) *n.* the use of words or expressions considered unacceptable
exertions (ig zur′ shənz) *n.* laborious or perceptible efforts

In each group of words below, circle the word that does **not** belong to the group. Use a dictionary if you need help.

1. offensive, uncivilized, polite

2. exertions, labor, rest, effort

3. disagreed, fought, reconciled, quarreled

EXERCISE C   Responding to the Selection

In persuasive writing, you try to convince your audience to have the same feelings, attitudes or opinions about a specific topic that you do. "Be Ye Men of Valor" is considered persuasive writing. Did Churchill's speech convince you? Write a short paragraph summarizing your answer. Use two selection and additional vocabulary words. Use the back of this sheet.

UNIT 6

Vocabulary Development

The Demon Lover ELIZABETH BOWEN

Selection Vocabulary

prosaic (prō zā′ ik) *adj.* commonplace; ordinary
intermittent (in′ tər mit′ ənt) *adj.* alternately starting and stopping
precipitately (pri sip′ ə tāt lē) *adv.* without deliberation
emanate (em′ ə nāt′) *v.* to come forth from a source; to issue
impassively (im pas′ iv lē) *adv.* in an emotionless manner

EXERCISE A   Applying Meaning

Write the selection vocabulary word that best answers each question.

1. Which word would describe a light that blinks on and off? _____

2. Which word might describe something you do quickly or instinctively? _____

3. Which word might describe someone who acts coldly or without feeling? _____

4. Which word refers to normal, usual, everyday things? _____

5. Which word could describe how heat comes from a fire or light comes from the sun? _____

EXERCISE B   Responding to the Selection

On the back of this sheet or on another sheet of paper, write a brief personal response to this story. Use at least two vocabulary words.

UNIT 6

Vocabulary Development

Musée des Beaux Arts *and* The Unknown Citizen W. H. AUDEN

Selection Vocabulary

reverently (rev′ rənt lē) *adv.* respectfully; with deep affection or veneration
forsaken (fôr sāk′ ən) *adj.* deserted or lonely
sensible (sen′ sə bəl) *adj.* having good judgment or sound thinking

EXERCISE A   Applying Meaning

Write the selection vocabulary word that answers each question.

1. How might you describe something that has been left to fend for itself? _____

2. How would you describe something done courteously, with great care for
someone? _____

3. How might you describe someone who makes good decisions? _____

EXERCISE B   Classifying

Write the vocabulary word that best completes each group of related words.
Use a dictionary if you need help.

1. abandoned, alone, isolated, lonesome, _____

2. sound, sane, wise, smart, _____

3. holy, respect, care, affection, _____

EXERCISE C   Responding to the Selection

On the back of this sheet or on a separate sheet of paper, write a paragraph
explaining which of the two poems you prefer and why. Use two of the
selection vocabulary words.

UNIT 6

Vocabulary Development
A Shocking Accident GRAHAM GREENE

Selection Vocabulary

callousness (kalʹ ləs nəs) *n.* hardness in mind or feelings; insensitivity

commiseration (kə mizʹ ə rāʹ shən) *n.* a feeling or expression of sympathy; compassion

intrinsically (in trinʹ zik lē) *adv.* inherently; in its very nature

brevity (brevʹ ə tē) *n.* shortness in speech or writing

appease (ə pēzʹ) *v.* to bring to a state of peace or quiet; to satisfy

EXERCISE A Applying Meaning

Write the selection vocabulary word that answers each question.

1. Which word would describe feelings of sympathy for another person? _____

2. Which word describes the act of trying to calm someone? _____

3. Which word refers to someone who is cold or uncaring? _____

4. Which word describes traits you are born with? _____

5. Which word is the opposite of *length*? _____

EXERCISE B Classifying
Additional Vocabulary

convulsion (kən vulʹ shən) *n.* involuntary muscle contraction

obscure (əb skyoorʹ) *adj.* not easily noticed or recognized

apprehension (apʹ ri henʹ shən) *n.* feeling of fear about the future

Write the additional vocabulary word that best completes each group of related words. Use a dictionary if you need help.

1. dread, uneasiness, foreboding, _____

2. spasm, seizure, twitch, _____

3. hazy, vague, shadowy, _____

EXERCISE C Responding to the Selection

On the back of this sheet, write a paragraph explaining why it was so important to Jerome for people not to laugh when they learned how his father had died. Use at least three of the selection and additional vocabulary words.

UNIT 6

Vocabulary Development

Fern Hill *and* Do Not Go Gentle into That Good Night

DYLAN THOMAS

Selection Vocabulary

hail (hāl) *v.* acclaim; pay tribute to
spellbound (spel′ bound′) *adj.* fascinated; affected as if by enchantment
heedless (hēd′ lis) *adj.* careless; not paying attention
frail (frāl) *adj.* delicate; fragile

| EXERCISE A | Determining Meaning |

Write the selection vocabulary word that best completes each sentence.

1. The little girl was _____ and captivated by the circus acts.

2. The woman was terribly _____; she could barely rise from her chair.

3. The town will _____ his accomplishments and honor his bravery with a parade next month.

4. The reckless driver received a ticket because of his _____ behavior.

| EXERCISE B | Practice with Synonyms |

Additional Vocabulary

grave (grāv) *adj.* very serious
bay (bā) *n.* a body of water
holy (hō′ lē) *adj.* something considered sacred or deserving of reverence

Write the additional vocabulary word that is a synonym (word with nearly the same meaning) for the word or phrase in bold type.

1. The peaceful **inlet** was lined with white beaches and thick pine forests. _____

2. Native people considered the palm tree **sacred**, and they punished anyone who needlessly chopped one down. _____

3. Fortunately, Alex's injuries were not **severe**. _____

| EXERCISE C | Responding to the Selection |

On the back of this sheet, write a paragraph describing which of the two poems you liked better and why. Use two of the selection and additional vocabulary words.

UNIT 6

Vocabulary Development

At the Pitt-Rivers PENELOPE LIVELY

Selection Vocabulary

benign (bi nīn′) *adj.* pleasant and friendly
explicit (eks plis′ it) *adj.* plainly and clearly expressed; definite
compulsory (kəm pul′ sər ē) *adj.* obligatory; required
radiant (rā′ dē ənt) *adj.* beaming, as with joy, love, or energy
envious (en′ vē əs) *adj.* feeling jealous or discontented because of the good
   fortune or superior abilities of another

EXERCISE A Determining Meaning

Write the selection vocabulary word that best completes each sentence.

1. The young girl looked glowing and _____ as she ran down the
   beach.

2. I have always found our town librarian to be a _____ and gentle
   person.

3. When my cousin got a new car for graduation, I felt spiteful and _____.

4. There were four _____ dives we had to complete to qualify for
   the final competition.

5. I thought the directions were fairly _____, but several people
   could not understand them.

EXERCISE B Applying Meaning

Write the vocabulary word that could replace the word or phrase in bold type
in each sentence.

1. Ken felt **disgruntled** because Jake, who was ten years younger, had a nicer
   home than he did. _____

2. Please be as **overt and blatant** as possible. I want to make sure I understand
   everything perfectly. _____

3. The bride looked **healthy and joyful** as she danced at the reception. _____

4. Attendance at the meeting is **mandatory**; anyone who misses it will be
   dismissed from the organization. _____

EXERCISE C Responding to the Selection

On the back of this sheet, use three vocabulary words to write a paragraph
giving your opinion of the narrator of "At the Pitt-Rivers."

Vocabulary Development
Wind TED HUGHES

flounder (floun′ dər) *v.* struggle to obtain footing
luminous (lo͞o′ mə nəs) *adj.* emitting a glowing light
grimace (grim′ is) *n.* a look of pain or disgust

EXERCISE A	Determining Meaning

Write the selection vocabulary word that best completes each sentence.

1. Her _____ told of the pain she experienced.

2. The bride's face was absolutely _____ with a megawatt grin as she walked toward her future husband.

3. My father warned me that I would _____ in the huge waves.

EXERCISE B	Classifying

Additional Vocabulary

stampeding (stam pēd′ ing) *v.* scattering suddenly
vanish (van′ ish) *v.* to pass from sight
tremble (trem′ bel) *v.* to shake involuntarily

Write the vocabulary word that best completes each group of related words.
Use a dictionary for help.

1. disappear, fade away, go, _____

2. quiver, shake, shudder, _____

3. charging, rushing, hurrying, _____

EXERCISE C	Responding to the Selection

On the back of this sheet, use three selection and additional vocabulary words
to summarize the main idea of Hughes's poem.

Vocabulary Development
A Mild Attack of Locusts DORIS LESSING

Selection Vocabulary

acrid (ak′ rid) *adj.* burning, biting, or irritating to the taste or smell
emphatically (em fat′ ĭ kəl lē) *adv.* in an insistent manner
irremediable (ir′ ĭ mē′ dē ə bəl) *adj.* not subject to remedy or cure
imminent (im′ en ənt) *adj.* about to happen; impending

EXERCISE A   Determining Meaning

Write the selection vocabulary word that best completes each sentence.

1. The error was _____; there was no way to repair the damage it caused.

2. The _____ fumes from the rotting materials made our eyes tear.

3. The staff prepared for the _____ changes because they had been warned that the new boss planned to redo all procedures.

4. The principal spoke _____ as he explained the new school rules to the assembly.

EXERCISE B   Classifying
Additional Vocabulary

exasperating (ig zas′ pə rāt′ ing) *adj.* causing irritation or annoyance
foliage (fo′ lē ij) *n.* a cluster of leaves, flowers, and branches
distorted (dis tôrt′ əd) *adj.* twisted out of a natural or normal shape
stoke (stōk) *v.* to poke or stir up
loathsome (lōth′ səm) *adj.* disgusting

Circle the word in each group that does not belong.

1. foul, loathsome, repulsive, shiny

2. exasperating, painful, soothing, frustrating

3. douse, dampen, stoke, snuff

4. garden, foliage, sky, tree

5. distorted, fake, mangled, misshapen

EXERCISE C   Responding to the Selection

On the back of this sheet, use three selection and additional vocabulary words to write advice for someone experiencing some kind of trauma or disaster. What would they need to survive such an event?

Vocabulary Development

The Train from Rhodesia NADINE GORDIMER

Selection Vocabulary

vendor (ven′ dor) *n.* one who sells goods
career (kə rēr′) *v.* to move or run with a swift headlong motion; to rush or dash along
wryly (rī′ lē) *adv.* in a twisted or distorted manner
sinew (sin′ u) *n.* a tendon

EXERCISE A   Applying Meaning

Write the selection vocabulary word that best answers each question.

1. How might someone smile if he or she doesn't mean it? _____

2. What is connected to muscles? _____

3. What does a galloping horse do? _____

4. What is a shopkeeper? _____

EXERCISE B   Determining Meaning

Additional Vocabulary

valance (val′ əns; vā′ ləns) *n.* drapery hung along the edge of a bed, table, canopy, or shelf
atrophy (at′ rəfē) *v.* to go slack; to weaken

Write the additional vocabulary word that completes each sentence.

1. If you don't use a muscle for a long time, it will begin to _____.

2. Iris thought the lacy _____ that hung around the table was stuffy and unnecessary.

EXERCISE C   Responding to the Selection

On the back of this sheet, use three selection and additional vocabulary words to write a paragraph describing the people and surroundings of the train station in the story.

Vocabulary Development

Dead Men's Path CHINUA ACHEBE

Selection Vocabulary

pivotal (piv′ ət əl) *adj.* of central or vital importance

denigration (den′ ə grā′ shən) *n.* defamation of one's character or reputation; slander

superannuated (soo′ pər an′ ū āt′ əd) *adj.* out of date

eradicate (ī rad′ ə kāt) *v.* to remove or destroy completely; to eliminate

EXERCISE A — Determining Meaning

Write the selection vocabulary word that best completes each sentence.

1. The _____ by her colleagues that Hilary suffered eventually forced her to leave her job.

2. To _____ some diseases is practically impossible.

3. Jeff was surprised that his aunt's _____ car still worked.

4. The birth of Sarah's child was a _____ experience for her.

EXERCISE B — Understanding Denotation and Connotation

Additional Vocabulary

designate (dez′ ig nāt) *v.* to indicate and set apart for a specific purpose

sceptical (skep′ ti kel) *adj.* having an attitude of doubt in general or toward a particular object

posture (pos′ char) *n.* the position or bearing of the body

Determine whether the additional vocabulary word in each sentence has a positive, negative, or neutral connotation.

1. Good **posture** is important for general well-being. _____

2. David was of a **sceptical** nature; he rarely believed something without first checking the evidence. _____

3. Do you think we should **designate** one person to design the posters? _____

EXERCISE C — Responding to the Selection

On the back of this sheet, use three vocabulary words to write a paragraph describing the attitude the schoolteacher in the story has toward the native people.

Vocabulary Development

Telephone Conversation WOLE SOYINKA

rancid (ran′ sid) *adj.* having an offensive or foul odor or taste

revelation (re′ ə lā′ shən) *n.* the act of making something known; something that is revealed

assent (ə sent′) *v.* to agree to something after consideration; concur

friction (frik′ shən) *n.* the clashing between two people or groups of opposed views

---

EXERCISE A | Applying Meaning

Write the selection vocabulary word that answers each question or that best completes the sentence.

1. What is telling someone a secret? _____

2. How might you describe rotten food? _____

3. What is a conflict? _____

4. You _____ to a plan when you decide to go along with it.

EXERCISE B | Practice with Synonyms and Antonyms

Additional Vocabulary

premises (prem′ is əz) *n.* a building or part of a building

emphasis (em′ fə sis) *n.* force or intensity of expression that gives importance to something

On the line, write whether the pairs of words are synonyms (words with nearly the same meanings) or antonyms (words with nearly opposite meanings).

1. premises/property _____

2. emphasis/accent _____

EXERCISE C | Responding to the Selection

On the back of this sheet, use two vocabulary words to write a paragraph describing an imagined meeting between the two characters in the story.

Vocabulary Development

Two Sheep JANET FRAME

Selection Vocabulary

gambol (gam′ bəl) *v.* to run, skip, or leap about in play; to frolic
pall (pôl) *n.* an atmosphere of dark and gloom
barren (bar′ ən) *adj.* having little or no vegetation; bare
unperturbed (un′ pər tûrbd′) *adj.* undisturbed; not troubled

EXERCISE A   Determining Meaning

Write the selection vocabulary word that best completes each sentence.

1. In winter the hills are quite _____, though they are full of greenery in the summer.

2. Mike was _____ when he missed the train since another was coming in a few minutes.

3. The lambs loved to _____ in the sunny fields.

4. Leslie disliked going down to the basement at night because of the _____ that filled the rooms.

EXERCISE B   Using Context Clues

Additional Vocabulary

luxurious (lug zhoor′ ē əs) *adj.* of the finest and richest kind
slyly (slī′ lē) *adv.* in a manner displaying cleverness
foe (fō) *n.* enemy

Use the context of each sentence to determine the meaning of the additional vocabulary word.

1. After sleeping outdoors during a camping trip, sleeping in a bed can seem delightfully **luxurious**.
   A. uncomfortable   **B.** boring   **C.** fancy

2. Derek hoped that his cousin would make up with him and stop treating him like a **foe**.
   A. friend   **B.** enemy   **C.** superior

3. Karen **slyly** figured out the solution to the riddle faster than anyone else.
   A. brilliantly   **B.** hastily   **C.** cheerfully

EXERCISE C   Responding to the Selection

On the back of this sheet, use two vocabulary words to write a paragraph summarizing the selection.

Vocabulary Development

from Tales of the Islands DEREK WALCOTT

Selection Vocabulary

precipice (pres′ ə pis) *n.* a very steep or overhanging mass of rock as on a cliff
fidelity (fil del′ ə tē) *n.* the quality or state of being faithful

EXERCISE A   Determining Meaning

Write the selection vocabulary word that best completes each sentence.

1. Dogs are animals known for their _____.

2. The _____ that jutted out over the water was an unsafe place to walk.

EXERCISE B   Classifying

Additional Vocabulary

twine (twīn) *n.* a strong string of two or more strands twisted together
glint (glint) *v.* to give off reflection in brilliant flashes

Write the vocabulary word that best completes each group of related words.
Use a dictionary for help.

1. thread, cord, yarn, _____

2. gleam, wink, shine, _____

EXERCISE C   Responding to the Selection

On the back of this sheet, use two selection and additional vocabulary words to
write a paragraph describing an island setting.

Vocabulary Development

B. Wordsworth V. S. NAIPAUL

Selection Vocabulary

hospitable (hos′ pi tə bəl) *adj.* offering generous and cordial welcome to
  guests
constellation (kon′ stə lā′ shən) *n.* any of eighty-eight groups of stars,
  many of which traditionally represent characters and objects in ancient
  mythology
patronize (pā′ trə nīz′) *v.* to become a customer of
distill (dis til′) *v.* to extract the essence of

EXERCISE A   Determining Meaning

Write the selection vocabulary word that best completes each sentence.

1. Three stars that are part of the _____ Orion are easy to
   recognize.

2. Anna is a very _____ hostess; she makes her visitors feel at
   home.

3. When making paint from natural materials, a person may have to
   _____ the materials to get a strong color.

4. The children were eager to _____ the new ice cream store.

EXERCISE B   Understanding Connotation

Additional Vocabulary

punctually (pungk′ chōō əl lē) *adv.* on time; in a timely manner
squat (skwot) *v.* to crouch close to the ground

Determine whether the additional vocabulary word in each sentence has a
positive, negative, or neutral connotation.

1. Maria had to **squat** to look through the basement window. _____

2. David's rehearsals always began **punctually**. _____

EXERCISE C   Responding to the Selection

On the back of this sheet, use two selection and additional vocabulary words to
write a paragraph that summarizes the main idea of the selection.

Vocabulary Development

Games at Twilight ANITA DESAI

Selection Vocabulary

stridently (strīd' ənt lē) *adv.* in a harsh, grating manner
defunct (di fingkt') *adj.* no longer existing or active; dead
temerity (tə mer' ə tē') *n.* excessive or reckless boldness; rashness
fray (frā) *n.* a heated dispute or contest
lugubrious (loo goo' brē əs) *adj.* excessively mournful or sorrowful

EXERCISE A   Applying Meaning

Write the selection vocabulary word that answers each question.

1. What is something that is old and forgotten? _____

2. How might you describe a very sad person? _____

3. What is a wild argument? _____

4. How might a person argue for a point? _____

5. What is going too far with bravery or self-confidence? _____

EXERCISE B   Practice with Synonyms

Additional Vocabulary

formation (fôr mā' shən) *n.* the manner in which a thing is formed; structure
frantic (fran' tik) *adj.* marked by fast and nervous or anxiety-driven activity
melancholy (mel' ən kol' ē) *adj.* depressed in spirits; sad
crucial (kroo' shəl) *adj.* important or essential in resolving a crisis

Choose the correct synonym for the additional vocabulary word used in each sentence.

1. Stephanie made a **frantic** search when she realized she'd lost her ticket.
  A. frenzied   **B.** calm   **C.** timely   **D.** suitable

2. The assistance of the Coast Guard was **crucial** in rescuing the people from the shipwreck.
  A. unnecessary   **B.** helpful   **C.** essential   **D.** indispensible

3. Gerard had a **melancholy** expression on his face after losing the tournament.
  A. triumphant   **B.** joyful   **C.** relaxed   **D.** sorrowful

4. The leaves of that tree have an unusual **formation**.
  A. base   **B.** shape   **C.** stem   **D.** growth

EXERCISE C   Responding to the Selection

On the back of this sheet, use three vocabulary words to write a paragraph describing the children from this story.

UNIT 7

Vocabulary Development
Elegy for the Giant Tortoises MARGARET ATWOOD

Selection Vocabulary

withering (wi th′ ər ing) *v.* becoming dry; shriveling from lack of moisture
periphery (pə rif′ ər ē) *n.* the outward or farthest boundary
plodding (plod′ ing) *v.* walking heavily and/or slowly
lumbering (lum′ bər ing) *v.* moving heavily and clumsily
obsolete (ob′ sə lēt′) *adj.* no longer in use; outdated

EXERCISE A Determining Meaning

Write the selection vocabulary word that best completes each sentence.

1. We stood on the _____ of the field, watching the game from afar.

2. In the morning, she comes _____ out of her room, looking for her coffee.

3. Eight-track cassette players are now _____.

4. The horses were tired as they went _____ down the road.

5. I haven't watered my plant in three weeks and now it is _____.

EXERCISE B Applying Meaning

Additional Vocabulary

awkward (ôk′ ward) *adj.* performed gracelessly; without coordination
paralyzed (par′ ə lizd′) *adj.* deprived of voluntary movement; unable to move
useless (ūs′ lis) *adj.* unusable; unsuccessful; inept

Write the additional vocabulary word that answers each question.

1. What word describes someone who cannot move part of his or her body? _____

2. What word describes something that no longer serves any purpose? _____

3. What word describes something unpleasant or gawky? _____

EXERCISE C Responding to the Selection

On the back of this sheet, use two vocabulary words to write a paragraph describing the tortoises in Atwood's poem.

Answer Key
British Literature, Unit 1, Adapted

from Beowulf

EXERCISE A: Determining Meaning

1. writhing
2. shroud
3. infamous
4. lament
5. forged

EXERCISE B: Practice with Synonyms

1. C
2. A
3. B

The Seafarer

EXERCISE A: Applying Meaning

1. blanch
2. flourish
3. rancor
4. admonish

EXERCISE B: Using Context Clues

1. C
2. A
3. B
4. C

from The Ecclesiastical History of the English People

EXERCISE A: Determining Meaning

1. diligently
2. frivolous
3. aspire
4. expound

Exercise: Classifying

expound: expand; explain; develop
diligently: industriously; thoroughly; attentively
aspire: seek; aim; desire
frivolous: silly; thoughtless; trivial

EXERCISE C: Responding to the Selection

Answers will vary but should include four sentences that incorporate two selection vocabulary words. Sentences should refer to an historical fact, event, or person.

from The Canterbury Tales, from the Prologue

EXERCISE A: Determining Meaning

1. disdainful
2. discreet
3. estimable
4. prevarication
5. solicitous

EXERCISE B: Classifying

1. C
2. E
3. A
4. B
5. D

EXERCISE C: Responding to the Selection

Answers will vary but should incorporate three selection vocabulary words and describe some of the characters.

from The Canterbury Tales, from The Pardoner's Tale

EXERCISE A: Determining Meaning

1. gratify
2. adversary
3. deftly
4. prudent

EXERCISE B: Determining Meaning

1. gratify
2. deftly
3. adversary
4. prudent

EXERCISE C: Responding to the Selection

Answers will vary. Summaries should use three vocabulary words.

from The Canterbury Tales, from The Wife of Bath's Tale

EXERCISE A: Determining Meaning

1. reprove
2. suffice
3. arrogance
4. disperse
5. concede

EXERCISE B: Practice with Synonyms

1. C
2. B
3. D
4. A
5. B

from The Book of Margery Kempe

EXERCISE A: Determining Meaning

1. restrain
2. slander
3. divulge
4. composure
5. instigation

EXERCISE B: Classifying

1. restrain
2. divulge
3. composure
4. instigation
5. slander

EXERCISE C: Responding to the Selection

Responses will vary. Paragraphs should incorporate three vocabulary words and discuss students' personal feelings about Margery Kempe's autobiography.

from Everyman

EXERCISE A: Determining Meaning

1. adversity
2. reckoning
3. respite
4. perceive

EXERCISE B: Practice with Synonyms and Antonyms

1. Synonym: weighing up/Antonym: disregard
2. Synonym: observe/Antonym: ignore
3. Synonym: break/Antonym: continuation
4. Synonym: hardship/Antonym: privilege

EXERCISE C: Responding to the Selection

Answers will vary. Summaries should include three vocabulary words.

from Sir Gawain and the Green Knight

EXERCISE A: Determining Meaning

1. dauntless
2. copiously
3. intrepid
4. blithe

EXERCISE B: Applying Meaning

1. indebted
2. gruesome
3. meager
4. peril
5. renowned

EXERCISE C: Responding to the Selection

Answers will vary. Paragraphs should use four vocabulary words and describe a knight's characteristics.

from Le Morte d'Arthur

EXERCISE A: Determining Meaning

1. peril
2. doleful
3. jeopardy
4. brandish

EXERCISE B: Understanding Homonyms

1. go away from
2. produce a likeness of
3. movement of air
4. just
5. pull out

EXERCISE C: Responding to the Selection

Answers will vary. Students should use three vocabulary words and describe a favorite character from the selection.

Sir Patrick Spens *and* Bonny Barbara *and* Get Up and Bar the Door

EXERCISE A: Determining Meaning

1. foremost
2. dwell

EXERCISE B: Applying Meaning

1. gay
2. tavern
3. deed

EXERCISE C: Responding to the Selection

Answers will vary. Paragraphs should use three vocabulary words and describe the setting of one ballad.

British Literature, Unit 2, Adapted

On Monsieur's Departure *and* Speech to the Troops at Tilbury

EXERCISE A: Determining Meaning

1. suppressed
2. valor
3. mute
4. concord
5. treachery

EXERCISE B: Classifying

1. stark
2. grieve
3. care

EXERCISE C: Responding to the Selection

Answers will vary but should include two vocabulary words in the summary.

The Lover Showeth How He Is Forsaken

EXERCISE A: Determining Meaning

1. meek
2. flee
3. bitter
4. stalking
5. continual

EXERCISE B: Determining Meaning

1. a large sum of money (answers may vary)
2. cell or room (answers may vary)

3. not wild; boring (answers may vary)

4. mean, hostile (answers may vary)

EXERCISE C: Responding to the Selection

Answers will vary. Students should include two vocabulary words in their rewritten endings to the poem.

Sonnet 30 and Sonnet 75

EXERCISE A: Determining Meaning

1. subdue

2. congeal

3. vain

4. mortal

EXERCISE B: Classifying

1. entreat

2. assay

3. delayed

4. devise

EXERCISE C: Responding to the Selection

Answers will vary. Students should use four vocabulary words in their descriptions of the main speaker.

Sonnet 31 and Sonnet 39

EXERCISE A: Determining Meaning

1. deem

2. balm

3. wan

4. scorn

5. languish

EXERCISE B: Responding to the Selection

Answers will vary. Students should use three vocabulary words to write their summaries.

Of Studies

EXERCISE A: Determining Meaning

1. sloth

2. impediment

3. discourse

4. execute

EXERCISE B: Applying Meaning

1. conference

2. rhetoric

EXERCISE C: Responding to the Selection

Answers will vary. Students should use three vocabulary words in their summaries.

Sonnet 116 and Sonnet 130

EXERCISE A: Determining Meaning

1. tempest

2. Tread

3. doom

4. alteration

EXERCISE B: Classifying

1. alteration

2. tempest

3. doom

4. tread

EXERCISE C: Responding to the Selection

Answers will vary. Students should use three vocabulary words when writing their descriptions of love.

Fear No More the Heat o' the Sun and Blow, Blow, Thou Winter Wind

EXERCISE A: Determining Meaning

1. folly

2. tyrant

3. censure

4. keen

EXERCISE B: Practice with Synonyms

1. C

2. A

3. B

EXERCISE C: Responding to the Selection

Answers will vary. Students should use three vocabulary words and discuss the speaker's experiences.

To be, or not to be, from Hamlet and All the world's a stage from As You Like It and Our revels now are ended from The Tempest

EXERCISE A: Determining Meaning

1. awry

2. pageant

3. calamity

4. infirmity

5. oblivion

EXERCISE B: Responding to the Selection

Answers will vary. Students should use five vocabulary words to paraphrase the main points from one of the speeches.

Macbeth, Act 1

EXERCISE A: Determining Meaning

1. plenteous

2. peerless

3. direful

4. repentance

5. prophetic

EXERCISE B: Determining Meaning

1. vanished
2. nature
3. deceive

EXERCISE C: Responding to the Selection

Answers will vary. Students should use four vocabulary words in their descriptions of Macbeth.

Macbeth, Act 2

EXERCISE A: Determining Meaning

1. provoke
2. stealthy
3. surfeited
4. predominance
5. scruple

EXERCISE B: Practice with Synonyms

1. B
2. E
3. D
4. C
5. A

EXERCISE C: Responding to the Selection

Answers will vary. Students should use five vocabulary words in their description of Macbeth's changes.

Macbeth, Act 3

EXERCISE A: Determining Meaning

1. incensed
2. appall
3. amends
4. indissoluble
5. jovial

EXERCISE B: Practice with Antonyms

1. D
2. B
3. C
4. A

EXERCISE C: Responding to the Selection

Answers will vary. Students should use four vocabulary words in their prediction of the action of Act 4 and Act 5.

Macbeth, Act 4

EXERCISE A: Determining Meaning

1. exploit
2. pernicious
3. redress
4. pertain
5. avarice

EXERCISE B: Practice with Synonyms

1. D
2. B
3. A
4. C

EXERCISE C: Responding to the Selection

Answers will vary. Students should use four vocabulary words in their descriptions.

Macbeth, Act 5

EXERCISE A: Determining Meaning

1. prowess
2. usurper
3. purge
4. antidote
5. siege

EXERCISE B: Determining Meaning

1. recorded
2. discovery
3. coward
4. revolt

EXERCISE C: Responding to the Selection

Answers will vary but should incorporate three of the selection and additional vocabulary words. The paragraphs should explain how the predictions of the Apparitions have come true in Act 5.

from Genesis and Psalm 23

EXERCISE A: Determining Meaning

1. enmity
2. abundantly
3. replenish
4. beguile

EXERCISE B: Practice with Synonyms

1. dominion
2. firmament
3. cleave
4. meat

EXERCISE C: Responding to the Selection

Answers will vary. Students should use three vocabulary words in their summaries.

Eve's Apology

EXERCISE A: Determining Meaning

1. discretion
2. endure

EXERCISE B: Classifying

1. C
2. A
3. D
4. B

EXERCISE C: Responding to the Selection

Answers will vary. Students should use three vocabulary words and agree or disagree with the speaker's ideas.

Song and A Valediction: Forbidding Mourning and Death Be Not Proud

EXERCISE A: Determining Meaning

1. refine
2. jest

EXERCISE B: Practice with Synonyms

Answers may vary, but should include appropriate synonyms for each selection vocabulary word.

EXERCISE C: Responding to the Selection

Answers will vary, but students should use one vocabulary word and discuss a simple idea's hidden meaning.

Meditation 17

EXERCISE A: Determining Meaning

1. congregation
2. Contemplation
3 covetousness

EXERCISE B: Determining Meaning

1. affliction
2. tolls
3. translated
4. mingled

EXERCISE C: Responding to the Selection

Answers will vary but should incorporate three of the selection and additional vocabulary words. The paragraph should discuss how the bell tolled to announce that someone was dying.

The Constant Lover and Why So Pale and Wan, Fond Lover?

EXERCISE A: Determining Meaning

1. spite
2. prevail
3. constant

EXERCISE B: Practice with Antonyms

1. B
2. D

EXERCISE C: Responding to the Selection

Answers will vary, but two of the selection and additional vocabulary words should be used in students' summaries.

To Lucasta, Going to the Wars and To Althea, from Prison

EXERCISE A: Determining Meaning

1. inconstancy
2. allaying
3. chaste
4. unconfined

EXERCISE B: Practice with Synonyms

1. accept
2. wonderful
3. opponent
4. cherish

EXERCISE C: Responding to the Selection

Answers will vary, but should incorporate three of the selection and additional vocabulary words. The paragraph should discuss Lovelace's attitude towards love, referring to specifics from one of the two poems.

To His Coy Mistress

EXERCISE A: Applying Meaning

1. strife
2. hue

EXERCISE B: Responding to the Selection

Answers will vary. Students should use three vocabulary words in their description of a relationship with a friend.

British Literature, Unit 3, Adapted

from Paradise Lost

EXERCISE A: Determining Meaning

1. discern
2. subterranean
3. deluge
4. myriad
5. transgress

EXERCISE B: Classifying

1. horrid
2. wrath
3. rebellious
4. vengeance

EXERCISE C: Responding to the Selection

Answers will vary but should incorporate four of the selection and additional vocabulary words. Paragraphs should describe a time students felt torn between good and evil.

from The Pilgrim's Progress

EXERCISE A: Determining Meaning

1. indictment
2. reconciled
3. diverse

EXERCISE B: Responding to the Selection

Paragraphs will vary. Students should describe the main events of *The Pilgrim's Progress* and use three vocabulary words.

On Her Loving Two Equally

EXERCISE A: Determining Meaning

1. subdue
2. mourn
3. passion

EXERCISE B: Responding to the Selection

Answers will vary but should incorporate three of the selection and additional vocabulary words. Paragraphs should also reflect students' personal opinions regarding the subject.

from An Essay of Dramatic Poesy

EXERCISE A: Determining Meaning

1. superfluous
2. esteem
3. insipid
4. monarch
5. bombast

EXERCISE B: Using Context Clues

1. B
2. A
3. C
4. C
5. B

from The Diary of Samuel Pepys

EXERCISE A: Determining Meaning

1. quench
2. cavalcade
3. malicious
4. loath

EXERCISE B: Applying Meaning

1. scaffold
2. magnificent
3. canopy
4. fling
5. ado

EXERCISE C: Responding to the Selection

Paragraphs will vary but should use four of the selection and additional vocabulary words and describe a festive event.

A Modest Proposal

EXERCISE A: Determining Meaning

1. deference
2. sustenance
3. digress

EXERCISE B: Understanding Archaic Usage

Answers will vary; some possible options are listed below:

1. dam: a structure retaining a body of water (Hoover Dam)
2. dear: something precious, a term of endearment
3. service: beneficial work; possibly military service
4. receipts: what you receive after paying for something

EXERCISE C: Responding to the Selection

Answers will vary. Paragraphs should summarize Swift's ideas and use three of the selection or additional vocabulary words correctly.

from Gulliver's Travels

EXERCISE A: Determining Meaning

1. magnitude
2. conjecture

EXERCISE B: Practice with Synonyms

1. avarice
2. apprehend
3. fortnight

EXERCISE C: Responding to the Selection

Answers will vary. Students should describe their favorite parts of the excerpt, using two vocabulary words.

Epigrams *and from* An Essay on Man

EXERCISE A: Applying Meaning

1. disabuse
2. commend
3. discord

EXERCISE B: Applying Meaning

1. err
2. skeptic
3. prey
4. stoic

EXERCISE C: Responding to the Selection

Answers will vary. Paragraphs should use three selection or additional vocabulary words correctly and discuss students' agreement or disagreement with Pope.

from The Rape of the Lock

EXERCISE A: Determining Meaning

1. confound
2. stratagem

EXERCISE B: Applying Meaning

1. vow
2. inscribe
3. rash
4. sprite
5. foe

EXERCISE C: Responding to the Selection

Answers will vary. Students should summarize the poem, using three selection and additional vocabulary words correctly.

Letter to Her Daughter

EXERCISE A: Determining Meaning

1. diversion
2. elate
3. edifice
4. inveterate

EXERCISE B: Classifying

1. inveterate
2. elate
3. edifice
4. diversion

EXERCISE C: Responding to the Selection

Answers will vary but should incorporate two vocabulary words. Paragraph should describe the advice student would give to a theoretical daughter or son.

from The Spectator

EXERCISE A: Determining Meaning

1. negligence
2. irrational
3. complaisance

EXERCISE B: Applying Meaning

1. irrational
2. negligence
3. complaisance

EXERCISE C: Responding to the Selection

Answers will vary. Paragraph should be a response to Steele's article about Sir Roger. Response should agree or disagree with the opinions Steele expresses in his article and use two vocabulary words.

from A Journal of the Plague Year

EXERCISE A: Determining Meaning

1. defy
2. confining
3. prodigious
4. oppressed

EXERCISE B: Classifying

1. oppressed
2. prodigious
3. confining
4. defy

EXERCISE C: Responding to the Selection

Answers will vary but should incorporate two vocabulary words. Paragraph should compare and contrast Defoe's narrative to another piece of historical fiction the student has read.

from A Dictionary of the English Language

EXERCISE A: Determining Meaning

1. aggregated
2. intuitive
3. vigilance
4. exultation
5. immutability

EXERCISE B: Classifying

1. syntax
2. longevity
3. obscurities

EXERCISE C: Responding to the Selection

Answers will vary but students should provide detailed explanations on why they chose the words they did and the influence the words have on them. Paragraphs should include three vocabulary words.

from The Life of Samuel Johnson

EXERCISE A: Determining Meaning

1. zealous
2. precept
3. ingenuity
4. veneration
5. impetuous

EXERCISE B: Applying Meaning

1. scoundrel
2. disposition
3. conviction

EXERCISE C: Responding to the Selection

Interview questions will vary but should incorporate three of the selection and additional vocabulary words. Students should write at least five questions.

Elegy Written in a Country Churchyard

EXERCISE A: Determining Meaning

1. pomp
2. genial
3. inevitable
4. uncouth
5. kindred

EXERCISE B: Practice with Synonyms

1. unavoidable
2. coarse
3. cordial
4. resembling

EXERCISE C: Responding to the Selection

Answers will vary but should include at least three vocabulary words. Paragraphs should address the imagery used in the selection.

John Anderson, My Jo and To a Mouse and Auld Lang Syne

EXERCISE A: Determining Meaning

1. bleak
2. foresight
3. dominion

EXERCISE B: Classifying

1. helplessness
2. hindsight
3. appreciative

EXERCISE C: Responding to the Selection

Answers will vary but should include at least two vocabulary words. Students should comment on their emotional reactions to the poems.

from A Vindication of the Rights of Woman

EXERCISE A: Determining Meaning

1. condescend
2. faculty
3. indignation
4. congenial
5. rational

EXERCISE B: Practice with Antonyms

1. D
2. A
3. B
4. C

EXERCISE C: Responding to the Selection

Answers will vary. Students' summaries of the selections should include at least three vocabulary words.

from The Diary of Fanny Burney

EXERCISE A: Determining Meaning

1. profound
2. confound
3. zenith
4. droll
5. sanguine

EXERCISE B: Applying Meaning

1. sanguine
2. profound
3. droll

EXERCISE C: Responding to the Selection

Answers will vary but should include two vocabulary words. Students' diary entries should describe a meaningful or important day in their lives.

from Pride and Prejudice

EXERCISE A: Determining Meaning

1. acquaintance
2. hypocritical
3. emphatic

EXERCISE B: Applying Meaning

1. vexed
2. universally
3. disposition
4. conceited

EXERCISE C: Responding to the Selection

Answers will vary but should include at least two vocabulary words. Students should describe specific qualities of the character they find the most appealing or interesting.

The World is Too Much with Us and It Is a Beauteous Evening, Calm and Free and My Heart Leaps Up and Composed Upon Westminster Bridge, September 3, 1802

EXERCISE A: Determining Meaning

1. piety
2. sordid

EXERCISE B: Classifying

1. majesty
2. eternal
3. outworn

EXERCISE C: Responding to the Selection

Answers will vary but should include at least two vocabulary words. Paragraphs should describe students' views on nature.

Lines Composed a Few Miles Above Tintern Abbey

EXERCISE A: Determining Meaning

1. repose
2. secluded

EXERCISE B: Determining Meaning

1. inland: of, relating to, or located in the interior of a country or region
2. plots: small pieces of ground
3. vagrant: wandering; erratic; uncertain
4. genial: pleasant and cheerful; friendly
5. hermit: one who lives a solitary life

EXERCISE C: Responding to the Selection

Answers will vary; students should use at least two vocabulary words in their explanations of the poem's meaning.

The Rime of the Ancient Mariner

EXERCISE A: Determining Meaning

1. impart
2. penance
3. dismal

EXERCISE B: Practice with Synonyms

1. B
2. C
3. A

EXERCISE C: Responding to the Selection

Answers will vary but should include at least two vocabulary words. Students should describe their reactions to the events and images in the selection.

from The Introduction to Frankenstein

EXERCISE A: Determining Meaning

1. relinquish
2. acute
3. illustrious
4. incite
5. transient

EXERCISE B: Applying Meaning

1. B
2. C

EXERCISE C: Responding to the Selection

Answers will vary but should include at least two vocabulary words. Students' paragraphs should include specific details about the story they have chosen.

She Walks in Beauty and from Childe Harold's Pilgrimage

EXERCISE A: Determining Meaning

1. spurn
2. mar
3. arbiter

EXERCISE B: Classifying

1. mar
2. arbiter
3. spurn

EXERCISE C: Responding to the Selection

Answers will vary. Students should include two vocabulary words in four sentences describing what they like about nature.

Ozymandias and Ode to the West Wind and To a Skylark

EXERCISE A: Determining Meaning

1. satiety
2. cleave
3. dirge
4. Tumult

EXERCISE B: Practice with Synonyms

1. B
2. C
3. D
4. A

EXERCISE C: Responding to the Selection

Answers will vary. Using two vocabulary words, students should summarize one of Shelley's poems.

La Belle Dame sans Merci and When I Have Fears That I May Cease to Be

EXERCISE A: Determining Meaning

1. glean
2. teeming
3. loitering

EXERCISE B: Applying Meaning

1. withered
2. relish
3. anguish

EXERCISE C: Responding to the Selection

Answers will vary but should include two vocabulary words. Students should explain which poem they like more and cite specific reasons why.

Ode on a Grecian Urn

EXERCISE A: Determining Meaning

1. desolate
2. deities

EXERCISE B: Practice with Synonyms

1. lament
2. container
3. people

To Autumn

EXERCISE A: Determining Meaning

1. conspiring
2. furrow

EXERCISE B: Applying Meaning

1. hue
2. mellow
3. reaped

EXERCISE C: Responding to the Selection

Answers will vary. Students' summaries should include at least two vocabulary words.

British Literature, Unit 5, Adapted

from In Memoriam A. H. H. and Crossing the Bar and Tears, Idle Tears from The Princess

EXERCISE A: Determining Meaning

1. redress
2. license
3. feigned
4. diffusive
5. sloth

EXERCISE B: Understanding Analogies

1. C
2. A
3. A
4. C

EXERCISE C: Responding to the Selection

Answers will vary but should incorporate four vocabulary words into a paragraph comparing one's own response to difficulties in life to that of Tennyson.

Ulysses

EXERCISE A: Determining Meaning

1. abide
2. prudence

EXERCISE B: Using Context Clues

1. B
2. C
3. A

EXERCISE C: Responding to the Selection

Answers will vary but should incorporate three vocabulary words into a descriptive paragraph regarding an aspect of the journey.

Pied Beauty and Spring and Fall: To a Young Child

EXERCISE A: Determining Meaning

1. blight
2. fallow
3. dappled

EXERCISE B: Classifying

1. blight
2. dappled
3. fallow

EXERCISE C: Responding to the Selection

Answers will vary but should incorporate two vocabulary words into a paragraph describing their feeling about spring and fall.

from Jane Eyre

EXERCISE A: Determining Meaning

1. retaliation
2. advocate
3. subside
4. vacant
5. scrutiny

EXERCISE B: Classifying

1. pity
2. honesty
3. great

EXERCISE C: Responding to the Selection

Answers will vary but should incorporate four vocabulary words into a descriptive paragraph regarding Eyre or Mr. Brocklehurst.

My Last Duchess

EXERCISE A: Determining Meaning

1. trifling
2. countenance
3. munificence

EXERCISE B: Applying Meaning

1. courtesy
2. rarity
3. earnest

EXERCISE C: Responding to the Selection

Answers will vary but should incorporate four vocabulary words into a paragraph discussing the student's perception of the duchess based on the speaker's conclusions.

from Oliver Twist

EXERCISE A: Determining Meaning

1. inseparable
2. philosophical
3. demolition
4. extraordinary

EXERCISE B: Classifying

1. excited
2. expert
3. clueless
4. spoke
5. insensitive

EXERCISE C: Responding to the Selection

Answers will vary but should incorporate five vocabulary words into a paragraph discussing a moment in the student's life when he or she followed a rule.

To an Athlete Dying Young *and* When I Was One-and-Twenty

EXERCISE A: Determining Meaning

1. threshold
2. rue
3. fleet

EXERCISE B: Practice with Synonyms

1. A
2. C
3. C

EXERCISE C: Responding to the Selection

Answers will vary but should incorporate two vocabulary words into a paragraph discussing a missed opportunity.

British Literature, Unit 6, Adapted

A Cup of Tea

EXERCISE A: Determining Meaning

1. exotic
2. quaint
3. odious
4. retort

EXERCISE B: Practice with Synonyms

1. vivid
2. dullness
3. sturdy
4. insult

Miss Youghal's Sais

EXERCISE A: Determining Meaning

1. farce
2. suppressing
3. unsavory
4. compensation

EXERCISE B: Determining Meaning

1. native
2. prying
3. initiated
4. agony

EXERCISE C: Responding to the Selection

Answers will vary but should incorporate two selection and two additional vocabulary words. Essays should comment on Strickland's English background as a reason why Miss Youghal's parents disapprove of him.

Shooting an Elephant

EXERCISE A: Applying Meaning

1. labyrinth
2. supplant
3. despotic
4. garish
5. squalid

EXERCISE B: Understanding Word Origins

1. C
2. B
3. A
4. D

EXERCISE C: Responding to the Selection

Answers will vary. Paragraphs should describe students' responses to the situation in the story and use two selection and additional vocabulary words.

Dreamers

EXERCISE A: Determining Meaning

1. feud
2. fatal
3. destiny

EXERCISE B: Understanding Analogies

1. A
2. C

Dulce et Decorum Est

EXERCISE A: Determining Meaning

1. trudge
2. vile
3. ecstacy

EXERCISE B: Practice with Synonyms

1. stand
2. helping

Sailing to Byzantium *and* The Second Coming

EXERCISE A: Determining Meaning

1. anarchy
2. vex
3. artifice
4. conviction

EXERCISE B: Classifying

1. fowl
2. slouches
3. gaze

EXERCISE C: Responding to the Selection

Answers will vary. Sentences should incorporate two selection vocabulary words and discuss personal escapes.

Preludes

EXERCISE A: Determining Meaning

1. infinitely
2. constituted

EXERCISE B: Applying Meaning

1. grimy
2. withered
3. dingy

EXERCISE C: Responding to the Selection

Answers will vary but should incorporate two of the selection and additional vocabulary words. Paragraphs should also address students' personal opinions regarding the subject.

The Rocking-Horse Winner

EXERCISE A: Determining Meaning

1. reiterate
2. obstinately
3. emancipate
4. parry

EXERCISE B: Responding to the Selection

Answers will vary. Sentences should incorporate two of the selection and additional vocabulary words and address Paul's family and money.

Araby

EXERCISE A: Determining Meaning

1. amiability
2. converge
3. impinge

EXERCISE B: Applying Meaning

1. amiability
2. impinge
3. converge

EXERCISE C: Responding to the Selection

Answers will vary but should incorporate two of the selection vocabulary words. Paragraph should describe an epiphany or minor realization the student has experienced.

from A Room of One's Own

EXERCISE A: Applying Meaning

1. hinder
2. morbid
3. guffaw
4. thwart
5. dilemma

EXERCISE B: Practice with Synonyms

1. A
2. C
3. B
4. D

EXERCISE C: Responding to the Selection

Answers will vary but should incorporate two of the selection vocabulary words. Paragraph should describe the student's feelings about Virginia Woolf's role in the battle for women's rights.

from Mrs. Dalloway

EXERCISE A: Determining Meaning

1. ailment
2. solemn
3. cordial
4. Presumably
5. perpetual

EXERCISE B: Classifying

1. dejected
2. vitality
3. bellow

EXERCISE C: Responding to the Selection

Answers will vary but should incorporate two of the selection and additional vocabulary words in descriptions of Mrs. Dalloway.

Be Ye Men of Valor

EXERCISE A: Determining Meaning

1. grapple
2. imperious
3. ravage
4. indomitable

EXERCISE B: Classifying

1. polite
2. rest
3. reconciled

EXERCISE C: Responding to the Selection

Answers will vary but should incorporate two of the selection and additional vocabulary words. Paragraphs should address students' personal opinions about the speech.

The Demon Lover

EXERCISE A: Determining Meaning

1. intermittent
2. precipitately
3. impassively
4. prosaic
5. emanate

EXERCISE B: Responding to the Selection

Answers will vary. Students should incorporate three of the selection and additional vocabulary words in their personal responses.

Musée des Beaux Arts *and* The Unknown Citizen

EXERCISE A: Applying Meaning

1. forsaken
2. reverently
3. sensible

EXERCISE B: Classifying

1. forsaken
2. sensible
3. reverently

EXERCISE C: Responding to the Selection

Answers will vary but should incorporate two selection vocabulary words. Paragraph should explain which of the two poems the student prefers and why.

A Shocking Accident

EXERCISE A: Applying Meaning

1. commiseration
2. appease
3. callousness
4. intrinsically
5. brevity

EXERCISE B: Classifying

1. apprehension
2. convulsion
3. obscure

EXERCISE C: Responding to the Selection

Answers will vary but should incorporate three of the selection and additional vocabulary words as possible. Paragraphs should also address Jerome's reaction to people laughing.

Fern Hill *and* Do Not Go Gentle into That Good Night

EXERCISE A: Determining Meaning

1 spellbound
2. frail
3. hail
4. heedless

EXERCISE B: Practice with Synonyms

1. bay
2. holy
3. grave

EXERCISE C: Responding to the Selection

Answers will vary but should incorporate two of the selection and additional vocabulary words. Paragraphs should also address students' personal opinions regarding the poem they liked better.

British Literature, Unit 7, Adapted

At the Pitt-Rivers

EXERCISE A: Determining Meaning

1. radiant
2. benign
3. envious
4. compulsory
5. explicit

EXERCISE B: Applying Meaning

1. envious
2. explicit
3. radiant
4. compulsory

EXERCISE C: Responding to the Selection

Answers will vary but should include a paragraph describing the student's opinions toward the narrator of the selection. The paragraph should incorporate three vocabulary words.

Wind

EXERCISE A: Determining Meaning

1. grimace
2. luminous
3. flounder

EXERCISE B: Classifying

1. vanish
2. tremble
3. stampeding

EXERCISE C: Responding to the Selection

Answers will vary but should summarize the main idea behind the poem. Three vocabulary words should be incorporated into the summary.

A Mild Attack of Locusts

EXERCISE A: Determining Meaning

1. irremediable
2. acrid
3. imminent
4. emphatically

EXERCISE B: Classifying

1. shiny
2. soothing
3. stoke
4. sky
5. fake

EXERCISE C: Responding to the Selection

Answers will vary but should incorporate three vocabulary words into a well-organized piece of advice.

The Train from Rhodesia

EXERCISE A: Applying Meaning

1. wryly
2. sinew
3. career
4. vendor

EXERCISE B: Determining Meaning

1. atrophy
2. valance

EXERCISE C: Responding to the Selection

Answers will vary but should incorporate three vocabulary words into a descriptive paragraph regarding the train station in the selection.

Dead Men's Path

EXERCISE A: Determining Meaning

1. denigration
2. eradicate
3. superannuated
4. pivotal

EXERCISE B: Understanding Denotation and Connotation

1. positive
2. negative
3. neutral

EXERCISE C: Responding to the Selection

Answers will vary but should incorporate three vocabulary words into a descriptive paragraph regarding the schoolteacher's attitude toward the native people.

Telephone Conversation

EXERCISE A: Applying Meaning

1. revelation
2. rancid
3. friction
4. assent

EXERCISE B: Practice with Synonyms and Antonyms

1. synonyms
2. synonyms

EXERCISE C: Responding to the Selection

Answers will vary but should incorporate two vocabulary words into a descriptive paragraph about an imaginary meeting between the selection's characters.

Two Sheep

EXERCISE A: Determining Meaning

1. barren
2. unperturbed
3. gambol
4. pall

EXERCISE B: Using Context Clues

1. C
2. B
3. A

EXERCISE C: Responding to the Selection

Answers will vary but should incorporate two vocabulary words into a summary of the selection.

from Tales of the Islands

EXERCISE A: Determining Meaning

1. fidelity
2. precipice

EXERCISE B: Classifying

1. twine
2. glint

EXERCISE C: Responding to the Selection

Answers will vary but should incorporate two vocabulary words into a descriptive paragraph about an island.

B. Wordsworth

EXERCISE A: Determining Meaning

1. constellation
2. hospitable
3. distill
4. patronize

EXERCISE B: Understanding Denotation and Connotation

1. neutral
2. positive

EXERCISE C: Responding to the Selection

Answers will vary but should incorporate two vocabulary words into a summary of the selection's main ideas.

Games at Twilight

EXERCISE A: Applying Meaning

1. defunct
2. lugubrious
3. fray
4. stridently
5. temerity

EXERCISE B: Practice with Synonyms

1. A
2. C
3. D
4. B

EXERCISE C: Responding to the Selection

Answers will vary but should incorporate three vocabulary words into a descriptive paragraph regarding the children of the selection.

Elegy for the Giant Tortoises

EXERCISE A: Determining Meaning

1. periphery
2. lumbering
3. obsolete
4. plodding
5. withering

EXERCISE B: Applying Meaning

1. paralyzed
2. useless
3. awkward

EXERCISE C: Responding to the Selection

Answers will vary but should incorporate two vocabulary words into a descriptive paragraph regarding the tortoises.